Other books by Dan Jones:

Words for Our Feelings: A Concise and Practical Guide to the Names for the Various Moods, Emotions, Sensations and Feelings

The Roller Coaster Kid Finds His Way Home (a nonconformist guide to happiness)

WHAT MAKES A MAN A MAN
AND OTHER TRUE ACCOUNTS OF MEN

INCLUDING

Why Men Don't Cry
A Brief History of Men's Work
What Makes Men So Tough
False Trails for Heroes

BY
DAN JONES

Published by Mandala Books and Tapes
P.O. Box 5892
Austin, Texas 78763
ISBN 0-9638104-0-5

Book and cover design by
Bill Jeffers Desktop Design and Production.

Printed on recycled paper.

for Albert Jones
1907-1992
good voyaging, Dad

and for all fathers and sons everywhere

Contents

Editor's Introduction

I remember being a boy watching my father rise from the breakfast table and lean over to kiss my mother goodbye as he left for work. "Well, I'm off to the salt mines," he would say. Always. That's what he always said and what I always heard. It was the 1950s. We lived in suburbia in a new brick house. My father wore a suit and I had no idea what a salt mine was, but it sounded terrible. I knew my father was making a joke because I had been to his office and it didn't appear terrible. Staid and boring, perhaps, but not terrible. So every day my father rose from the table, jauntily kissed my mom and made a joke about the next nine hours of his life.

In that repeated experience lay many of my early lessons about "what makes a man a man." Men leave the home; men's work is tedious; humor forestalls desperation; heroism lay not in dynamic creativity but in stoic acceptance of duty. I learned thousands of other lessons, of course, from many, many sources. Necessarily, every culture greatly exerts itself teaching its young men and women what it expects of them. And just as necessarily, adults also remind themselves what is expected of their lives, while we kids listen in and imitate. Long ago we told stories orally—some of them surviving to become the great national epics; nowadays, our television programs, movies, commercials, music videos, and books serve the same purpose. The health of our families, communities, nations, and planet depends on the stories and metaphors we use to explain our Selfs to ourselves and to our children. And one reason that our families, communities, and nations become abusive, hopeless, weak, rigid, fearful, and ineffective is that the stories we tell ourselves are so.

As Dan Jones mentions, our problem as men and women these days is not the lack of stories and models. Rather there are, perhaps, too many. And a large number of them are failing us. Sometimes our stories fail us because the original circumstances that engendered the stories have changed so that the stories become inappropriate: stories from a nation at war may not enlighten the same nation at peace; the stories that make me a good boss may not make me a good father. And sometimes changing circumstances blind us to positive aspects of older, fading stories. My lone wolf heroes of the 1960s—from the movies of Steve McQueen, Al Pacino, and Jack Nicholson—tarnished the tales of forbearing and forgiving fathers—from the television programs of Fred McMurray, Andy Griffith, and Robert Young.

In this slim volume, Dan Jones performs a miracle of literary, anthropological, psychological undercover work. The sheer number of stories that he has read in preparation for this book is amazing. The geographical and cultural range of these stories—from Greece to China to Argentina to Scandinavia—is astounding. More astonishing, however, is the palpable transformation these stories and their characters go through in Dan's care.

Unlike Carl Jung, Joseph Campbell, Robert Bly, Robert Moore, and Doug Gillette, Dan refuses to dehumanize the heroes of the old stories. Jung and his descendants teach us much, but they search the old tales for their mythic qualities—in essence, distancing us from the men and women who people them. In their hands, Odysseus becomes an archetype whose story we may and may not participate in. In other words, today when I read *The Odyssey*, I may learn who I am by finding in myself a pale reflection of Odysseus.

Dan subtly yet dramatically alters our perspective by demythologizing—that is, humanizing —the men and women of the old stories. Assuming that the stories teach us how to be human, Dan explores, instead, the characters' behaviors, thoughts, and emotions, asking how the stories teach us to be, act, and feel more completely and more fully. In this way, Dan can ask the question the "mythic" Odysseus provokes: What grief in my life am I experiencing? And he can ask a new question: Why does Odysseus cry but none of the men I know cry? From other stories, he can ask why men suppress emotions and when it is beneficial to do so and when it is not. In still other stories, he can inquire about behaviors and emotions that once were useful and now are not.

I was fortunate to attend the workshop in February 1992 that is the foundation for this book. Over the course of a weekend in Austin, Texas, Dan alternated experiential exercises and discussion with presentations of the information contained here. This book, rewritten and adapted from taped recordings of that workshop, conveys the power, intelligence, fortitude, and integrity that Dan instills into his every act. As you read this book, imagine Dan's bright face, his infectious smile, and his happily graceful body standing before you and forty of your friends. He holds in his hands not one note. Everything you are about to hear—including many lengthy passages from the world's favorite stories—flow from his generous memory in his melodious and supple voice.

When I listen to Dan, when I read his books, I am reminded that I need not limit my life, my manhood, to a meaningless acquiescence to familiar necessity. I may choose to leave my home each morning, but my work, whatever it is, need not be slaving in a salt mine. Part of a long tradition of men devoted to husbandry, I can understand the power of my decisions and gladly feel all the emotions contained in that life. Part of another long and great tradition, Dan is a very human—and manly—teacher.

Lyman Grant
Editor and Publisher
MAN! Magazine

Preface: Masculine Tradition

The most challenging thing today about knowing how to be a man is that we have not too little but way too much information about it, and much of what we have is contradictory and confusing. So what we need is not so much new information as it is a good sorting out of all the old information so we can—each man in his own way—choose to leave behind the less healthy things, like emotional repression, rescuing damsels, and villainizing other men, while keeping the parts we love, like courage, and skill, and honor.

This book is also written very much for women, so you can see what our traditions are, how much they mean to us, and what the difficulties are that we are working our way through. There is, of course, obviously nothing about courage, and skill, and honor that excludes women, and there are millions of women and children who are right now living lives of great heroism. But just as women are intelligently sorting out their own unique traditions, so we men are doing the same with our unique traditions, so that we can come back together as better and more understanding friends and allies.

To find out what I mean by "the old traditions," and to see what this whole book is based on, take a look at pages 93–103. Here is the roll of heroes and sages and bards that boys are taught to admire—the men who fought the great battles, slew the monsters, sailed the uncharted seas, settled the frontiers, journeyed to the lands beyond the living. Often these men are treated as mere action figures. But here in this book, we will demythologize them, and discover the real value behind the actions of their stories, the value that makes a man a man.

These men are mythologized in another sense as well, by being idealized into supermen, or treated as archetypes and paradigms, which sometimes leaves them up on a lofty perch without much human ground under them. We will demythologize them in this sense also, and see them as real and individual men behind the myths, with intense inner emotional lives, less concerned with being models and symbols than with their own often volatile and conflicting feelings. We will let them tell us who they really were and how they were like us; what they thought about their lives and how they felt about themselves; if they ever got scared doing all those brave deeds, and if they ever cried about it all; why they put themselves through the terrible ordeals, and what made it worth it for them. Here we can see them not as perfect models to be followed in every detail, but as men like ourselves, seeking to be worthy of us, their descendants, just as we seek to be worthy of our own children and grandchildren by keeping alive the greatest and most masculine of the old traditions.

Good luck to us all.

Dan Jones
Austin
1993

What Makes a Man a Man

What Makes a Man a Man

Every culture teaches its boys how to be men by using Teaching Stories. These stories typically present a hero who embodies and defends the ideals of the people—caped crusaders, valiant knights, masked riders of the plains, and all manner of dauntless derring-doers. Boys are expected to absorb these stories and practice them in play, until we have internalized and identified with the ideals of the people. In some degree, for bad or good, this has happened to us all.

What is it that these stories teach us? What does our culture expect us to learn and to do?

The stories are highly action-oriented in order to keep the attention of boys, so on the surface it appears that we're supposed to be doing things. But actually, the actions have a significance beyond themselves, and it is this significance that our culture wants us to absorb.

Furthermore, in the lives of real heroes, the great actions are few and far between, yet the hero is always a hero, and the reason is not that he once did something but that he stands for something. A man is a hero not because he's on a winning team, but because his team stands for something. A man who wins but doesn't stand for much is treated not with respect, but with scorn or pity. (We can all think of examples from politics, business, and sports.)

So what is it that our culture wants us to stand for? And how do we do that?

First, according to all the traditions of masculinity from all history and every part of the world, what we stand for is an ideal, like Freedom, or Justice, or Peace, that is much larger than ourselves; and opening our lives to that ideal is what makes our lives grow and expand to "larger than life," and gives us an inner sense of quiet confidence.

Second, we accomplish this by possessing certain personal qualities, and by placing these qualities in the service of our ideals and of our people.

1. Personal Qualities

A survey of the tales of heroes from all over the world and from all ages of history shows many different personal qualities, but only four that are universal, as though you couldn't have a hero without at least a little of all four of these:

Prowess
Savvy
Courage
Honor

Not all heroes have all of these in equal measure, but every hero (unless he's a tragic one) has enough of each one, and specializes in one or two. In the stories, a man who has the first three but lacks Honor is a villain; has three but lacks Courage is a coward; has three but lacks Savvy is a fool; has three but lacks Prowess is a flop. Fortunately, all of these qualities can through practice be developed by every man.

Prowess can take any of these forms:
Skill
Strength
Endurance
Skill in a warrior hero usually means skill with a weapon: Robin Hood's bow and arrow, Wyatt Earp's quick draw. There are also nonwarrior heroes with other kinds of skills: athletic, technical (astronauts), medical, rhetorical, political, et cetera.

Strength means anything in the direction of Hercules wrestling with monsters, or Samson pushing down the pillars of the temple.

Endurance is a quality especially useful to explorers, and the greatest tales of endurance are the ones like those of the Australian Douglas Mawson's lonely and terrifying trek across the ice chasms of Antarctica, or of the mountain man Hugh Glass, so horribly mauled by a grizzly bear that his companions left him for dead with no food or weapon, who crawled 200 miles to the fort.

Strength and endurance can also be psychological and spiritual, as many heroic tales have told, which is good fortune to men who are not too excited about being warriors.

Savvy can take these forms:
Quick Wits
Resourcefulness
Wisdom in Council
The original hero with Savvy was Homer's *Odysseus*, who was the best at council during the Trojan war and then traveled around the world living by his wits.

A hero who specializes in this is called Trickster. Trickster appears especially among people who are oppressed and powerless, who cannot safely display prowess because of the oppression. The great American Trickster, who emerged from black slavery, is B'rer Rabbit. This is why another oppressed group, children, who live in a world of B'rer Foxes and B'rer Bears, instantly identify with B'rer Rabbit.

Courage can take these forms:
Daring
Determination
Cool under Pressure
Life on the Line
Courage means "overcoming fear." It does not mean being fearless. Whenever a hero is said to be fearless, or without fear, or knows not the meaning of the word, it is almost always some third person describing the hero, not the hero himself. Also, these unreal descriptions turn up typically in comic books and cheap fiction, not in the great epics. From ancient Homer's heroes ("green fear took hold of them"); to King Arthur's knights sharing their fears with each other; to Davy Crockett, in his autobiography, talking about how "scared" he was in the earthquake, and once when he was lost in the woods at night, and once out on the Mississippi River, or, what was his worst fear, giving a speech ("set my knees to shakin' and my heart to flutterin'");* to Kit Carson, in his autobiography, saying he was "never so badly scared

* Sources for quotations are given in the *Notes* section beginning on page 85.

in my life" as when those two grizzly bears started after him. In every corner of the heroic world, including the greatest, hands tremble, hearts pound, knees go weak, voices choke, hair stands on end. But men go on and do it anyway—that's Courage.

> *Honor* has these forms:
> Honesty
> Integrity
> Loyalty
> Generosity
> Fair Play

Honesty means truth-telling; Integrity is staying true to your word. These two, plus Loyalty mean that you are a reliable man, a sound man, your comrades can count on you in any danger, you are trusted by other people of Honor. Nathan Hale. George Washington. The men who signed the Declaration of Independence, pledging "our Lives, our Fortunes, and our sacred Honor."

Generosity. Among the old stories are many about a hero who liberates a treasure from some dragon or giant; but the point of having the treasure is to become known as a great giver of gifts—gold armbands and rings and magical swords—this was a big part of your fame, and minstrels gave long sections of their heroic songs to telling how generous you were. Native Americans have a saying: the braver a man is, the more he gives away. Heroes can also be generous with their time and skills.

We all know the code of Fair Play. No hitting a man in the back; no kicking him when he's down. No fair two picking on one. No hitting below the belt. Turn about is fair play. Don't be a sore loser. These sorts of things are not written down in any code book. We learned them as boys on the playground, and as men we play business and politics by the same code, or risk being seen as villains or cowards.

This code comes down to us from the most ancient tales. The oldest of them all, the Sumerian epic, *Gilgamesh*, from the third millenium B.C., is largely about how an arrogant king learns to deal justly with his people. The oldest and most influential of all the western epics, Homer's *Iliad*, is essentially about the heroic code of honor, and the madness that happens when it breaks down. The *Odyssey* is about Odysseus regaining his integrity after it was destroyed in a savage war. All the great heroic stories tell us that men without honor are less than men. It is not just deeds, but how they are done.

When young Sir Cologreant rides out on his first knightly quest, he meets a giant who asks him what it is he seeks. "Some adventure," he replies, "whereby to test my prowess and my bravery." From Zaire comes a story that begins: "When Bassadjalan Zambele was young, he said to his father, 'I want to go to a far away land and prove my valor.'" (And men with the valor to seek the test generally have the valor to pass it.)

From all over the world there comes to us story after story of men testing their Prowess, Savvy, Courage, and Honor, the personal qualities that have traditionally made a man a man. Now to see how these qualities are used so that we stand for something more than just ourselves, and our lives expand with a full, deep richness.

2. Ideals

Every person, every family, every culture wants to feel secure, to prosper, and to be fulfilled. It is the job of the hero to create or preserve the conditions under which these things can happen—security, prosperity, and fulfillment.

To feel secure, there needs to be
Peace
Order
Justice
Freedom

These are the four classical ideals that heroes from the oldest times have stood for, and it is no accident that these four make up most of the Preamble to the United States Constitution.

To prosper, we need
Health
Wealth

To be fulfilled, we need
Beauty
Wisdom
Love

These nine, or ideas very similar, are the great ideals of culture, and a man who gives his life to the service of any one or more of them, for the benefit of the people, is called a hero.

Security. Among the oldest stories of heroes that have come down to us, there is a very high percentage that have to do with monster slaying. I know of no serious stories where a hero rides off to pick a fight with a peace-loving monster. Always the monster is laying waste the countryside, or causing a famine or a plague, or eating somebody. Monsters, by definition, represent the forces of chaos and darkness that threaten the security of the people. (In fact, if you took away Monsters, Invaders, Tyrants, and Bullies, there would be very little left of the whole body of heroic stories.) Monster-slaying heroes, by definition, represent the forces of order, peace, and justice that guarantee the security of the people.

Traditionally, it has been the social or political order that has been threatened. More recently, it has been the order of Nature, and heroes in Greenpeace and other organizations have been fighting to preserve the Natural Order.

Some cultures put less stress on Order and more on Freedom. In Scotland, for example, individual Freedom has always been at the heart of the people, and most of the stories that have come down from ancient and medieval Scotland are not about monsters but about the struggle for individual liberties and the right of the people to choose their own kings. In the middle ages, when the French knights came over to help one side or the other, and they rode their horses through the fields and trampled down the crops, they were astonished to see the peasant farmers chasing after them with hoes and pitchforks. No peasantry anywhere else in Europe would dare to do that to the nobility.

"Give me liberty or give me death" came from Patrick Henry, and Patrick Henry's father came from Scotland. The first wave of pioneers who pushed off from the Eastern seaboard were mostly Scotch-Irish, and they carried these values into the Allegheny Mountains, where they still flourish, and into the mountains of New Hampshire where all the license plates say "Live Free or Die."

Then as the frontier moved across the continent and there grew up all the stories about making the frontier safe for the settlers—this was all about Peace and Justice, about Freedom and Order. And of course the braves of the native tribes were defending the same ideals of their cultures, only they didn't have revolvers and Gatling guns.

Everywhere, all over the world, anytime a hero is doing battle with monsters, giants, aliens, invaders, outlaws, traitors, infidels, whatever—these are the forces of chaos, disorder, and darkness that threaten the survival, the security of his people. And he, the hero, stands for the life of Freedom and Order, of Peace and Justice, under which his people can survive and flourish.

Prosperity. The stories that boys grow up on, in the comic books and the TV shows, mostly feature heroes who guarantee the people's security against disorder: war, crime, violence, and fear. Soldiers and pilots, detectives and sheriffs.

But as we grow older, we learn that there are other arenas for us to act in. The people also fear disease, famine, and poverty, and so there are heroes of Health, who work out on the frontiers of medicine fighting deadly microbes: men like Louis Pasteur, and the discoverer of the polio vaccine, Jonas Salk.

There are also heroes of Wealth, philanthropists like Andrew Carnegie. But it cannot be overstressed in these days that the hero brings the treasure back to his people; the heroism of wealth is more in the giving than the getting. A man who accumulates wealth mainly for himself has the mark of a villain or a coward, and may find himself opposite a real hero like Robin Hood or Emiliano Zapata.

Fulfillment. It is not just the basics we need. We have made heroes of men who bring us Beauty: music, poetry, and art, from Beethoven to the Beatles, Shakespeare and Walt Whitman, Michelangelo and Van Gogh.

There are heroes of Wisdom and Truth: of science (Galileo), of philosophy (Socrates). The one great civilization that has no national epic and very little in the way of heroic stories is China. Collections of Chinese literature begin not with tales of the earliest warriors and explorers, as do the collections of most other civilizations, but with the works of Confucius and Lao Tzu. I surmise that this is because China has always valued the group more than the individual, and elders more than youngers, so they are not so likely to cherish stories of young men setting off on solitary adventures. Chinese literature is founded not in action but in Wisdom.

There are heroes of Love and Compassion. Jesus and Buddha. St. Francis. Gandhi. There's no lessening of Courage here, or of Prowess and Savvy, or of Honor. And no heroes ever stood for any greater ideal or brought more benefit to the people.

We have many arenas in which we can choose to work, and it is not the arena that defines heroism, nor the degree of outward success. It is the inner, personal qualities and the ideals that give a man a knowingness and a deep, relaxed confidence in himself, and that open the doors and windows of his life to something more than himself so that he expands to "larger than life." Any time a man is living his life with Courage, Prowess, Savvy, and Honor, and he places these qualities in service to a great ideal, and for the benefit of his people, whatever his success may be, then according to every standard that has ever been, without the slightest doubt, he is a Man.

3. What to Do

Our first enemy is the fear that we have to do it all alone. Men have always had comrades and have acted together in bands. Many men are finding that when we talk with other safe and honorable men about the challenges we face, our lives open up and change in good and powerful ways.

Our second enemy is the fear that some men are born heroes and some are not. With each other's help, we all can develop the qualities and find the ideals, and if we have been given any different ideas about ourselves, then we can track down those ideas to their sources and drive them out.

Our third enemy is the fear that we are at the mercy of circumstances. ("If only somebody would start to drown while I'm walking by the river, and I pull them out and get in the newspapers.") There are no shortages of needs for good men, and with each other's help, we can find and create our own circumstances.

In pairs and groups, men gather and talk about questions like these:

Who have been my heroes? as a boy? as a man? What were their ideals? What were their personal qualities? How did I absorb these qualities, develop these ideals?

Did my Dad have a code? (Grandad? Mom's side of the family?) Did he live it? Did he teach it? How has this code affected me?

Could the men in my family be heroes (have ideals and act on them with some confidence)? Could the women? children? elders? If not, why not? What do I need to say about this?

How have I lived with Prowess? with Courage? with Savvy? with Honor? as a child? as an adult? How do I practice these qualities? What are my ideals today? If I'm not sure, what would I like them to be?

What arena(s) for action suit me best? (public service; science/technology; business/economics; education; art/music/writing; politics; health; law; ministry; ecology; and not least, fathering)

What forms of Prowess, Courage, Savvy, and Honor best suit my arenas?

Who is a safe and honorable friend (or friends) to share this book with, so the two (or more) of us can talk these questions out among us? and support each other in becoming the real men who are inside every one of us, waiting to come out in full power and savvy and courage and honor?

Why Men Don't Cry

Why Men Don't Cry

Not a month goes by that doesn't bring another new medical study showing that men who express feelings are healthier, feel better, and live longer. Studies have shown that crying normalizes our testosterone levels, making us more masculine. Other studies show that emotional tears contain and carry off certain chemicals that are associated with depression, and others that are associated with mood swings and aggressive behaviors. In addition to this large body of objective evidence, there are increasing numbers of men who report that crying makes us feel better subjectively, and also think more clearly and rationally. So you would expect that men, rational, scientific creatures that we are, would at least begin to experiment with crying, right?

Not hardly. Large numbers of men would not even consider it. Other large numbers have gotten the message intellectually, but their best efforts will not bring tears. (Some of these men have serious medical problems, and they know that relearning to cry is a matter of critical importance for them.) Other large numbers of us have recovered the ability to cry, but sometimes when we do, a little voice says, "What would Davy Crockett say if he could see you like this?" or "John Wayne/your Dad/your buddies/the Lone Ranger?" The fear and shame of crying are so enormously strong that some of us would rather get sick and die than cry.

Sometimes it is alleged that real men don't cry and never have. This is a particularly nefarious belief, and therefore it is a great pleasure to be able to refute it and trounce it to smithereens. The truth is that the greatest warrior heroes from nearly every culture on earth always cried freely, openly, and unashamedly until about 200 years ago. The story is as follows.

The original and most influential heroic story in all of western culture is Homer's *Iliad*. Throughout it, not only do warriors cry openly when their friends are killed or wounded (because who wouldn't?), but the whole story—which is a tale of how a long and terrible war destroys the heroic code of honor, so that the early, courtly duels, where men show mutual respect and honor, degenerate into vaunting over the slaughter of supplicants and sleeping men—this whole story culminates and finds its resolution in the great scene where the opposing leaders, Achilles and King Priam, come to see each other as fellow suffering men, and cry deeply with each other ("the sound of their mourning moved in the house").

And in the *Odyssey*, the original, archetypal quest story in our culture, Odysseus, whom everybody says is the most cool-headed of all the Greeks, makes his first appearance crying. For seven years, he's been on the island of Calypso, a goddess who has promised him eternal youth if he will stay and be her lover; but he's been gone from his home and family for 20 years, and all he wants is to go home again, so he spends every day down on the coast looking out to see if any ship is coming, and the first words that describe him are: "wracked his heart with groaning . . . tear on tear brimming his eyes . . . scanning the bare horizon of the sea."

And when he finally makes it home and reunites with his son, Telemachus, whom he hasn't seen for 20 years, "helplessly they cried, pouring out tears." That is what men did, even the most cool-headed.

Now somebody might say: well, that was the Greeks, they were a passionate people, but those Romans, they were stoic, you won't find them crying. However, that is not the case. The great Roman hero, Aeneas, in Vergil's *Aeneid*, is the embodiment of Roman virtue, the great model whom Roman boys were taught to emulate, and in our first look at him he is in a great storm at sea, and fearful of disaster, he utters a lament. (Remember the "hero's lament"?) He weeps at the funeral of his friend, Pallas, and at Carthage, as he tells Queen Dido and her court the story of the fall of Troy, tears are pouring down his cheeks. In fact, throughout the *Aeneid* and the *Odyssey*, any time that horrific war is mentioned, every man in the room who was there breaks out in tears.

Historical Romans cried, too. Julius Caesar burst into tears of shame in front of all his men when he read that Alexander the Great had accomplished more at the same age than he had. Alexander also cried openly in front of his men.

In the very oldest epic that we have from anywhere, the Sumerian *Gilgamesh* from 2300 B.C., King Gilgamesh and his friends cry together when they're sad, they cry when they're afraid, they cry over the fate of mankind, that we have to die. When his best friend, Enkidu, dies, Gilgamesh cries for 7 days and 7 nights.

The taboo against crying in our culture is so strong that I thought it might come from the Bible, so I looked into the Old Testament only to find the great warrior kings crying. Saul cries tears of remorse when he learns he has suspected David falsely. David cries several times when he has to go into exile, and when he finds his city burned, and whenever his family or his friends are killed. If ever there was a military man, it was Joshua, and when he learns that some of his men have been killed, "Joshua rent his clothes and fell to the earth upon his face ... and said, 'Alas, O Lord God.'" So the taboo doesn't come from the Bible, and doesn't seem to come from anywhere around the ancient Mediterranean world.

In some cultures, men's tears are valued. In Russia, for example, the city of Smolensk was saved from a Mongol invasion by its great hero, Mercurius, and Mercurius was blessed with "the gift of tears." This meant that when he went into church to pray before the battle, as everyone did, he was able to cry from the beginning to the end of his praying. This was greatly admired. Other Russian heroes, including the greatest of them all, Alexander Nevsky, had "the gift of tears."

Native American warriors also cry in prayer, in the sweat lodge, opening and draining not just the sweat glands but also the tear glands, getting every kind of toxin out so as to be refreshed and open to a fresh vision; and on a quest, praying and crying for a vision, praying and crying for understanding.

Men's tears can change history. There is a story from Africa about a hero named Diuladjan, who was the great hero of the kingdom of Kiban. Kiban was in a war that had been going on for years with the kingdom of Tuba. Tuba had recently invaded, and now it was Kiban's turn to go back and invade. The invasion was set for the next day.

Diuladjan was one of those tremendous heroes, so great, like Hector of Troy, that the whole defense of the city is organized around him. The night before the invasion Diuladjan's two best friends come to see him, and they walk in and find Diuladjan weeping. They ask what's going on, and Diuladjan says these words:

> *I am crying because of the consequences of what we are about to do. We have great heroes and Tuba has great heroes and we shall fight and some of our heroes will no longer be alive. Who will be left to defend the Seven Cities? Our widows and orphans cannot do it. This war will bring Kiban to its downfall. That is why I am crying.*

His friends go and tell the chief, who calls the elders, and they have a council and talk this over and they agree: Diuladjan is right, this has been going on for too long. So they call off the war. No more widows and orphans. Because one great man cried.

The stories of heroes weeping, from cultures all over the world, are too numerous to tell, and it would tax the reader's patience to read all of even the most interesting ones. But rather than leave any of these out, I will provide headers so each reader can at least read something from his own cultural heritage, and then pick our story back up on page 30.

*   *   *

JAPAN. One culture I took a look at was the samurai, because I couldn't imagine samurai crying. And it's true, they don't cry over anything having to do with *giri*, or duty. If it's a matter of duty, a samurai never shows any sign of sorrow, fear, or regret. Ah, but when the emperor dies, "fierce warriors . . . weeping" all over the palace. When the emperor goes into exile, everybody going with him is weeping.

Samurai cry tears when their friends are killed, when they lose a lover; there are tears of regret, and tears of gratitude to a benefactor.

They had a saying back then in those old stories from medieval Japan, "His sleeve was soaked with tears." They had those big, full sleeves, and they put their forearm up to their forehead to give themselves a little privacy and then they would just let go and soak the sleeves with tears. I could sum it up this way. If you are a samurai and your general orders you on a suicide mission, you don't bat an eye. Your whole life has prepared you for this ultimate moment of glory. But if your general surrenders, the shame of that surrender, the disgrace, the sorrow are so overwhelming that you don't have enough sleeves in your wardrobe to hold all the tears. You and everybody around you all weeping.

NATIVE AMERICA. The braves were very, very stoic. They used to do things like roast sunflower seeds on the fire and then put them on the wrists of the boys and if a boy flinched, he was taunted with being a woman, so when he grew up and was in pain he would never show it. Oh, but when Crazy Horse died, men couldn't stop crying for days. And later, at the ghost dance, tears over the lost glory of the old days. There are times when it's okay.

South of the Rio Grande, Aztec heroes cry at partings and dyings and all the times when a man would want to cry. And the greatest of all their heroes, Quetzalcoatl, as he leaves his beloved city of Tula to go on his journey to the land of the dead, as he climbs up on a big boulder for one last look at his beloved city, he weeps tears that fall and break the heart of the stone.

In South America there was a culture called the Gaucho. These men were part Spanish, part native. They were nomads, living out on an immense desert of thorn bushes called the Pampas. They were hunters and horse breakers, and their whole culture was built around horses. Their clothes were horse-hide, and their furniture was horses' skulls. They were very jealous and they settled matters of honor with duels with a *facón*, a long double-edged blade half way between a dagger and a sword. Tough, tough hombres.

But in this same culture, it was considered a disgrace not to be able to play the guitar, and you made up your own songs and you sang your poem, your passion, you sang your joy and your sorrow. And when you sang your sorrow, tears rolled down your face, and everybody understood because they did the same thing. Their greatest hero, Martin Fierro, says:

> *You have to go through it (life)*
> *with all the suffering and tears,*

*cause nothing teaches you more
than to suffer and cry.*

ENGLAND. Germanic tribes who settled in England, the Angles and Saxons, left us an epic called *Beowulf*. When the monster, Grendel, comes up and eats some of the men in the mead hall, "many a man is brokenheartedly lamenting." When Beowulf is killed at the end, his men carry him off on their shoulders, tears streaming down their faces.

The stuff about the British and the stiff upper lip came later, much later. It was not there in the Middle Ages. It was not there at the time of the King Arthur stories. Whether these stories are written by an Englishman, Sir Thomas Malory, or by Chretien de Trois and the French writers, there are plenty of opportunities for heroes to weep, and they do and with each other.

The version I like is the one by Sir Thomas Malory, *Le Morte d'Arthur*, because Sir Thomas was himself a knight, a veteran of the Wars of the Roses. He also wrote his book while he was in prison for various offenses against the public order, so he was not any effete court poet, and when he talks about what knights feel inside, I trust him. If you were a knight in his story, you would cry when your friends are killed, when your friends are wounded, when your friends ride out on a quest because you don't know if you're going to see them again, and when they come back because you're so happy to see them again. You cry when war is declared, and you cry when peace breaks out because you are so relieved.

The last chapter of *Le Morte d'Arthur*, where everybody dies, is one enormous long lamentation. When Sir
Lancelot dies, the lamentation goes on for 15 days and
nights. And what's more, this is not just watery eyes. Sir
Thomas says tears "burst," "stream," "pour," "for a long
time," "all day and night." And another thing, when the
knights of King Arthur's round table weep over each
other's wounds, he uses the word, "tenderly." You get the
feeling from reading these stories that these men really
love each other.

This is not too surprising, when men live together and train together and especially when we share danger. A lot of men wouldn't use that word, "love," but that
really is what happens. There is a story about Sir
Lancelot, who was the greatest of all the knights for
prowess, and if there was a fight, he was The Man you
wanted on your side. Sir Lancelot was fought to a draw,
as far as I know, only once, and that was by Sir Tristram,
of the Tristram and Isolde story.

Sir Tristram and Sir Lancelot were the best of
buddies, but one day it befalls that Sir Lancelot enters
the forest from the east, traveling west, and Sir Tristram
enters the forest from the west, traveling east. For some
reason, they are not wearing their usual colors, and as
they approach they put down their visors and they don't
recognize each other. It's a narrow path, so there is a
question of which knight is going to give way to the
other, and they are proud knights and so words are
exchanged and then there is a challenge and before you
know it, they are bearing down on each other with their
lances. Well, they're both pretty good at this and they

unhorse each other. So then they take out their swords, those enormous, heavy broadswords, and commence to whacking on each other for four hours. At the end of which time, Sir Thomas tells us, they are both "wonderly sore."

About this time it occurs to them to ask, who is this guy, anyway? So they ask, and when they find out, they throw off their helmets and, in Sir Thomas' words, "either kissed other an hundred times."

Kissing may seem unusual to us, but in almost all heroic cultures in the world, heroes embrace, and in most of them, they kiss, usually on the cheek. In the Bible, when Saul sends David into exile, David's best friend is Saul's son, Jonathan, and they hate having to part so much that the Bible says, they "kissed one another and wept with one another." All the way back to the oldest epic we have, Gilgamesh and his friend, Enkidu, walk off to fight Humbaba ("whose name is Hugeness") holding hands. This is the way it has always been in most heroic cultures.

CELTIC. The same is true of the Celtic warrior bands in Ireland, Scotland, and Wales. When the much-loved hero Owein, whom all had given up for dead, suddenly returns, "Owein threw his arms around Arthur's neck, and they embraced. And with that his men came hurrying and pressing towards them to try and see Owein and embrace him, and very nearly were there dead men in that press." Celtic heroes cry when their friends are killed, when they're in prison or exile, when they're tired of wandering, and like men today who can cry at sad movies, they cry in the great hall when the minstrel sings a sad song.

GERMANY. The Germans are well known as tough and stoic. Their national epic is the *Nibelungen-lied*—that's the one where Wagner got the plots for his operas, and it's filled with the toughest guys you'd ever want to meet. But when Siegfried is killed, his friends weep for him. And then the whole *Nibelungenlied* leads up to this scene at the end where you have never seen such death before dishonor. Man after man walks out into nearly certain death rather than face the shame of not doing so. And after too much of this, suddenly the few survivors look around at the thousands of dead and realize what's happened, and there ensues the most terrific lamentation and weeping that I have ever read in any heroic literature anywhere in the world.

FRANCE. The great national epic is the *Song of Roland*. This is an eighth-century epic about repelling a Moorish invasion, and you have never seen so much weeping and swooning at dyings and partings of friends. When Roland's best friend, Oliver, dies, Roland weeps and the poem says, "Never in the world will you hear a more sorrowful man." And when Roland dies and his body is found at the end, 100,000 knights weep and throw themselves to the ground. King Charlemagne weeps and tears his beard out.

SPAIN. The great national epic of Spain is the *Poem of the Cid*. El Cid is the paragon of all Spanish chivalry and heroism. Single-handedly, he saved his country from a Moorish invasion, "up to the elbows in blood," exemplar of dignity and duty before self, control before passion.

Yet when he's sent into exile by the treacherous King Alfonso, as he rides off he turns for one last look at his beloved lands and tears are pouring down his cheeks. And soon after, when he has to leave his wife and children at the convent for their safety, the poem says

> *He turned and looked upon his daughters.*
> *"To God I commend you and to the Heavenly*
> *   Father;*
> *Now we part, God knows when we shall come*
> *   together."*
> *Weeping from his eyes, you have never seen*
> *   such grief,*
> *Thus parted the one from the others, as the nail*
> *   from the flesh.*

That is a scene that young Spanish heroes grew up on.

*   *   *

All across Europe, men weep, from the Portugese mariner-explorers to Eastern Europe's great Prince Marko to Russia's cossacks weeping for days at the death of the

Czar, "like a river flows, sobs like thunder rumbling." Around the world in every heroic culture, heroes weep at dyings and woundings and partings, in sorrow and in anger and in remorse. I could say it was universal in all the old heroic cultures if it were not for the single exception of the Vikings. Nowhere in any Viking saga can I find a lamentation, and almost never a tear. Even the women, as often as not, will not cry. Instead, when there's a death, everybody's first thought is, how can we get revenge for the murder of our kinsman? Viking sagas are family sagas and they are mostly about endless feuds back and forth between the families.

At first I thought the lack of emotion might have something to do with the climate—cold weather, cold feelings. But in the *Kalevala*, the great national epic of Finland, there is as much emotion as anywhere. The hero Ilmarinen fought bears and sorcerers and journeyed to the Land of Death, and when his wife died he cried "for weeks." And the greatest of all their heroes, the mighty Vainamoinen, when he was once lost in the woods alone at night, cried so loud they heard him across the lake. He was also their archetypal minstrel, and once he was out in a boat and he composed music that was so sad it made him cry and his tears fell and dropped into the lake and became blue pearls.

Another great Finnish hero, Lemminkainen, was the most reckless adventurer of all, and he wept bitterly, deep, and long when he had to leave the island where for three years every night a thousand maidens had vied for the right to sleep with him. (Well, I guess a lot of us might cry at that one.)

So Viking repression of emotions probably doesn't come from the climate, and I think the origins of it are probably lost in the mists of time. But the fact is that this is the only one of the old cultures I can find where there are no circumstances where a man can cry, and where men are actually taunted for crying. It also has few if any cultural rivals for being the most dark, pessimistic, and depressed, and for being the tops in alcohol consumption. (Connection?)

I tried to imagine an historical influence between their culture and ours, because of course what I want to know is how did all of us here in America today inherit this miserable, wretched, mind-numbing repression. I tried tracing it through Scandinavian immigration, and when that didn't seem very promising, I tried to see it coming from Viking conquests of Northern Scotland in the tenth century, the resulting intermarriages, and from there to America via the Scotch-Irish immigration. But alas for that theory, Robert Bruce and his men, the greatest of all the Scottish heroes, lived later on in the fifteenth century, and they had no trouble crying when they left home to go to war or when their friends were killed. So I gave up on finding a major Viking connection and looked elsewhere for the source. The answer came, surprisingly, from Southern Europe.

Our story begins in Italy in the year 1528, which saw the publication of a book called *The Courtier* by a soldier and diplomat named Baldassare Castiglione, and which became the rage among the nobility all over Europe. It consisted of a series of conversations about what a man of nobility should be like, and the gist of it was that in addition to being brave, strong, smart, and honorable, a man should also have a certain degree of Refinement.

In addition to being a man of action, he should also be a man of letters. His conversation should be learned, elegant, and witty. His manners should be polished, his clothes fashionable, his appearance pleasing to the ladies of the court. Now we can see that there was probably some room for refinement when we look into the etiquette books of the time and find advice like, "Don't blow your nose on the tablecloth," or "Spit not in the room, but in the corner." Also, "Do not relieve yourself in front of the ladies." So it could be argued that *The Courtier* had an improving effect on society, at least in its basic sanitation engineering.

But what happened then was that as time went on the idea of refinement became increasingly refined. This was particularly so in the institution of the French salon, which was created by the ladies of the French court in the early 1600s in an attempt to take some of the rough edges off the barons, and which was so successful that by the early 1700s, the ladies had become the arbiters and judges of elegance. These French ladies, some of whom were so refined that they would faint upon seeing a dog naked, had the gentlemen (note the word) wearing lace cuffs and shiny pants, powdered wigs and make-up to hide the blemishes, and competing with each other to see who could wear the most exquisite perfume.

In this atmosphere, the height of indiscretion was to show any emotion. Emotion was the very opposite of elegance. It involved loud noises and bodily fluids. Tears were in the same class with spit and with, pardon the expression, nasal discharge. Recall that this was a pre-Darwinian era when humans were thought to be in a different category from animals, and the similarities were embarrassing.

It was also the Age of Reason, when Reason was regularly contrasted with bestial instincts and emotions. Recall also that the nobility thought of themselves as being in a different category from the rest of humanity, a more exalted and elegant category, and here they had found a cunning way to distinguish themselves from the bourgeoisie and the peasantry by holding in their emotions. Also, men were now learning what women had known for centuries: when you cry, it causes your make-up to run and you look just a fright.

So 250 years ago, when holding in tears began to be fashionable, it did not at all mean being manly. It meant being well-mannered. It meant not offending polite society. Not crying was originally part of the sissification of men.

Now the question comes, how did this sorry business get from Parisian salons to us? Well, in a variety of ways, but principally by means of a book called *Lord Chesterfield's Letters to His Son*, which had a phenomenal popularity both in England and in the United States, and which became the inspiration and the ultimate authority for men's behavior in the rows and rows of etiquette books that swept over this country in the 1800s. If you could quote Chesterfield on etiquette, that ended all arguments.

Lord Chesterfield himself grew up in an atmosphere of elegance and worldly cynicism, and when he visited Paris, not only did he feel instantly at home in the salons, but he was accepted there as was no other Englishman. His career was diplomacy, and he was just a born natural at being elegant. In letter after letter to his son, he advises him to be cool and stoic. He writes:

> *Having mentioned laughing, I must particularly warn you against it. And I could heartily wish that you may often be seen to smile, but never heard to laugh while you live. It is the manner in which the mob express their silly joy at silly things. And they call it being merry. In my mind there is nothing so illiberal and so ill-bred as audible laughter. . . . Not to mention the disagreeable noise that it makes and the shocking contortion of the face that it occasions. . . . I am sure that since I have had the full use of my reason, nobody has ever heard me laugh.*

Nor did anyone ever see tears in Lord Chesterfield's eyes. Again he writes to his son:

> *Make yourself absolute master, therefore, of your temper and your countenance so far at least as that no visible change do appear in either, whatever you may feel inwardly.*

And finally, he writes:

35

> *It may be objected that I am now recommending dissimulation to you. I both own and justify it. Without some dissimulation, no business can be carried on at all.*

In his own day, Chesterfield was lampooned by the best writers of the time, Jonathan Swift and Dr. Johnson, both men of some emotion, but Chesterfield won the day in the etiquette books of Victorian England and America that our great-great-grandmothers pressed upon our great-great-grandfathers and upon their sons, our great-grandfathers, in a crusade to elevate these sons of democracy up to the level of the noble Lord Chesterfield. (Whose son, by the way, came to a bad end.)

Now the question comes, how did this French parlor etiquette get into the stream of heroic tradition, so that even a man like John Wayne holds back his tears like a French dandy trying to please the Countess? In Chesterfield's day, in the 1700s, the three great adventure tales that boys read were *Gulliver's Travels, Pilgrim's Progress*, and *Robinson Crusoe*. All three heroes, Gulliver, Christian, and Crusoe, when they cry, do so openly without any embarrassment, apology or explanation. Crusoe, for example, is very emotion-oriented. He cries for joy when he's saved from the storm; for sorrow, realizing all his shipmates are drowned; in despair at ever being rescued; in gratitude at finding the seed corn; most of all in prayer; and sometimes for no immediate reason. Crusoe says, "In the midst of the greatest composures of my mind, the feeling would break upon me like a storm and make me wring my hands and weep like a child.

Sometimes it would take me in the middle of my work and I would immediately sit down and sigh and look upon the ground for an hour or two together and this was still worse for me, for if I could burst out into tears or vent myself by words, it would go off and the grief, having exhausted itself, would abate."

So 250 years ago, men still knew that tears wash away grief. How did we lose this knowledge? In the 19th century, the old epic, which had always been the form in which we men expressed our heroism, faded away and was replaced by the adventure novel. And as we read the great adventure novels of the first half of the previous century by Scott and Dumas and Cooper, the new cultural models for masculinity, we encounter something we have rarely ever seen before outside of Viking culture: heroes are ashamed of crying. In Walter Scott's enormously popular *Ivanhoe*, heroes simply don't cry. King Richard, also known as the Black Knight, has, we are told at the start, "a careless gaiety and a fearless confidence." And that is just about all that we ever hear about his having any emotions at all. The same with Ivanhoe and Robin Hood. In the whole book, the only man who cries openly, without any embarrassment, is Wamba the Fool.

In other Scott novels, heroes will cry, but this is usually shown as a weakness, and the hero is embarrassed by it and tries to stop crying. In *The Three Musketeers*, D'Artagnan cries when he leaves home and later when his lady dies, but he makes efforts not to. And in this same book, the class origins of not crying show up clearly in the scene where Athos and M. Boniface, a haberdasher, or clothier, are ordered to the Bastille. Athos, an aristocrat in disguise, merely shrugs, while M. Boniface "sat there weeping like a real haberdasher."

Historians of the American western story trace its roots back to the novels of James Fenimore Cooper. In all five of the *Leatherstocking Tales, The Last of the Mohicans* and the rest, Hawkeye and Chingachgook and the other heroic figures cry seldom and when they do it is seen as a weakness to be ashamed of. Outside of Viking culture, this is new.

Well, that was the first half of the 19th century. In the second half, it gets worse. Increasingly, heroes are not allowed to cry at all. Robert Louis Stevenson, in *Treasure Island* and *Kidnapped*, allows his boys to cry, but not the men. And his even more popular rival, G. A. Henty, whose adventure tales sold 25 million copies to our great-grandfathers when they were boys, has his boys scorn other boys who cry. Henty himself was a British war correspondent who loved the job, and his biographer says of him that Henty had "a horror of any lad who displayed any weak emotion and shrank from shedding blood or winced at any encounter." A hundred years ago, our grandfathers and great-grandfathers grew up on this stuff, along with an enormous river of dime novels with titles like *Roaring Ralph Rockwood the Reckless Ranger*, where the heroes are mostly like Buffalo Bill who, we learn right at the start, "had learned to hide all his feelings," so he does everything "cool and collected."

If you read the journals and reminiscences of the old cowboys, you will find that cowboys almost never cry, unless their horse or dog dies, and usually not even then. Then, if you read the journals and reminiscences of the mountain men, you will find that mountain men may cry when their friends are killed, when they're rescued, at reunions with comrades, when they have to leave a lady love in St. Louis, when they have to leave the mountains to return to civilization.

Now I don't suppose that this was because cowboys were tougher than mountain men. If anything, mountain men faced greater and more constant danger than cowboys. But the heyday of the mountain men was from about 1820 to 1840, so these guys grew up before the Chesterfield etiquette had taken any deep root in America. The heyday of the cowboys, of the open range and the cattle drives, was from about 1870 to 1890. So these guys, the cowboys, grew up under the influence of the Walter Scott novels and the etiquette books. And thus, in not crying, they were being more civilized and acceptable to polite Victorian society.

If the general attitude toward crying in the 19th century was one of uneasiness and ambivalence, the matter was settled in 1902 with the publication of a book called *The Virginian* by Owen Wister. You may have seen the movie with Gary Cooper. It was *the* runaway best seller of the entire first decade of the 20th century, and it set the type for men for the next 90 years. The strong, silent type, tough and cool, holding in all his feelings. The Virginian does admit that there are two things that give him "a sensation of surprise"—lightning and marriage. At one point, when his old friend Steve is hanged, he is so "utterly overcome" with emotion that he just can't hold it in anymore, so what does he do? He talks it over with his horse.

Now whenever a book comes out with such phenomenal popularity as this one had, it creates a new market for more of the same, and there is never any shortage of writers who are eager to satisfy the market. The first two big names who figured out the formula were Zane Grey and Max Brand, who between them turned out hundreds and hundreds of stories with strong, silent type heroes who rarely showed any feelings.

The Hollywood screen writers were not slow to pick up on the new fashion in men, and they began giving us Bronco Billy and Tom Mix and Hopalong Cassidy. The next generation of writers that came up in the 1930s, led by Luke Short, and the next generation that came up in the 1950s, led by Louis L'Amour, just carried on this same foppish fashion. L'Amour wrote a book called *Hondo*, and it says on the cover:

> *Best book I've ever read.*
> John Wayne

So naturally I had to take a look at that one. We learn right off about Hondo that

> *there was no softness in him. His toughness was ingrained and deep, without cruelty, yet quick, hard, and dangerous. Whatever wells of gentleness might lie within him were guarded and deep,*

which is just about all we ever learn about him as a human being.

In the film *Cahill: U. S. Marshall*, John Wayne hears that his old friend, the sheriff, has died, and he says without a sign of emotion, "Well, I ain't gonna mourn him. He lived a good life." And guess what he does as he delivers these manly lines? He moves over to the sideboard and pours himself out a big glass of whiskey. Well, of course. That's how he was taught to handle his feelings by a tradition slightly older than himself.

Then, of course, came the TV script writers, who gave us *Gunsmoke* and *Bonanza* and *Wagon Train* and *Lawman* and *Rifleman,* and on and on. In 1958, the peak year, there were 37 prime-time westerns on TV for us to grow up on, at least five every night, and those of us whose masculinity was formed in this era were utterly saturated with these new-fangled strong, silent types, and with hundreds of breath-stopping scenes of the shaming of any man who showed his feelings. Is it any wonder that we're afraid of our own inner selves?

When the cowboy craze faded out, the same hero type just moved on into a new uniform. Now he was a police detective, an astronaut, a spy, but he was the Virginian over and over and over again. He was brave and strong and smart and honorable mostly, like the heroes of old, but his emotional roots are not in the heroic tradition at all. They are in the French salon. When a man holds in his feelings, it is not to show his courage, it is so he won't offend polite society with loud noises, facial contortions, and bodily fluids. A man holding back his tears is not being heroic, he is being a nice boy, ashamed to make a fuss, who doesn't disturb his Daddy and pleases his Mommy.

A final word on all this. As Dante, in the *Divine Comedy*, descends deeper and deeper into Hell, the sins of the sinners become worse and so do the punishments. After going down through fires and stenches and all kinds of horrible tortures, Dante at last comes to the bottom floor of Hell. There the very worst of all the sinners are frozen up to their necks in ice, and at the very bottom of the bottom, the very worst of the worst are frozen with their heads back so that the ice comes up around their eyes, and when they cry, the tears freeze and block the tear ducts so that no more tears can flow out. Dante says:

> *their very weeping closes up their eyes,*
> *and the grief that finds no outlet for its tears*
> *turns inward to increase their agonies.*

Holding in tears is the most cruel and horrible torture in Hell.

A Brief History of Men's Work

A Brief History of Men's Work

Anthropologists do not yet have enough data to tell us how long we men have been living on the earth. The latest figures are something like 700,000 years for homo sapiens, 1.5 million for homo erectus. We've had fire for a million and a half. So suppose we just take the biggest, roundest number available and say that we men have been living on the earth for a million years. And if you say that there is an average of 25 years in each generation, that means that there have been 40,000 generations come before us. Forty thousand levels back of great, great, great, great . . . grandfathers. And what, I wonder, were we men doing all that time?

Well, for 39,600 generations, we were all doing pretty much the same thing. Unless we had something to do with medicine, we were hunters and warriors, meaning that we provided for our families, and when we needed to, we protected our families. Hunter, warrior: provider, protector. And so, just by definition of the word, we were all heroes. The word *hero*, taken back through its Latin and Greek forms to the old Indo-European language, means "protector." Provider, protector: hunter, warrior. That was what we did for 39,600 generations. That was the job.

Then about 400 generations ago (about 10,000 years), there began what is called the Neolithic Revolution. What that essentially means is that some of us began to specialize. Instead of doing what all men did, we became farmers or shepherds, cowherds and goatherds, and a few of us became potters and weavers. And that is basically where things stayed for most of the next 200 generations—tribes living in villages where some of the men had specialties, but all shared in the daily communal life—until a little over 5,000 years ago, when the second wave of the Neolithic Revolution began and some of us became miners, metal workers, and wheelwrights, and others became masons, and we built walls around our villages, and inside the walls some of us became merchants and traders, officials and bureaucrats, priests and scholars, and professional warriors. With more specialization, we see less of each other and move farther apart.

That is pretty much the way things stayed until only about 15 generations ago, when a few of us began to become scientists and technologists. Only about eight generations ago did anybody start working in a factory or on a railroad, and it hasn't been but three generations since anybody was a truck driver, or a pilot, or an electrician. And for how long have we been computer and telecommunications specialists?

When I look at those numbers, the first thing I notice is the acceleration. 40,000, 400, 200, 15, 8, 3, 1. It makes you wonder what's around the corner. The other thing I notice is that ratio of 40,000 to 400. It would suggest that if each man is an evolutionary summation, then the hunter-warrior in us outnumbers all the rest 99 to 1. No wonder, in our efforts to change ourselves, we are having such a hard time letting go of this guy. We have his body, his endocrine system, his adrenal glands. In terms of evolution, 10,000 years is not a very long time.

What was life like for us back then, for 39,600 generations? What did it take for a man to be able to provide for and protect his family? Well, according to anthropologists, it seems that it took about 20 hours a week. This was usually concentrated into a big hunt that would last for two or three days, and if the hunt was successful, you could take a week off. What you would do during this week was, since you didn't get much sleep during the hunt, you would sleep a lot at night and then in the morning you would take a nap. And then in the afternoon you would take another nap. In between, you would spend some time socializing with your friends, but most of your time would be spent in spiritual work. Stone Age men wouldn't call it spiritual work because they didn't distinguish between secular and sacred (everything was sacred), but we would call it spiritual work: making art, for example, like the cave paintings, or the Navajo sand paintings, or the Australian aboriginal dream paintings. Also, music, drumming, and dancing. Anthropologists report that dancing is the single biggest activity during the week off. All these forms of spiritual work were designed to pull ourselves back together after the exhausting and dangerous hunt, and get ourselves back in harmony with the spirits, the gods, the ancestors, the animals, or whatever powers that be.

I do not want to romanticize Stone Age cultures because those guys were helpless in lots of ways that we're not. But still, when you look at that 20-hour workweek and then you look at the way our culture asks us to live, it's enough to set a man to thinking.

The great advantage to the Neolithic Revolution was that we could store a surplus, and that meant that when game was scarce or drought persisted, we wouldn't all die, which was a great advantage. But there were some disadvantages. The first is that farming and the other occupations are more labor intensive, and our 20-hour workweek begins to expand. At some seasons of the year especially, there is so much work to be done that some men specialize in it and come to be known as the men who do the work. The workers. And we have the beginnings of the working class. Also, with all this work to do, slaves become more valuable, so they become more numerous and we have a slave class.

The second disadvantage of the Neolithic Revolution is that a stored surplus is an inviting target for an enemy attack, so the bigger our surplus, the more defense we need. We have masons now, so we build walls around our villages, and then we have to man the walls, and we have to send out scouts to see who or what may be coming to raid our surplus. Most of us are too busy producing all this surplus to do the training that it takes to defend, so we need somebody to do that for us. Certain men look like they'd be good at it anyway, so we ask them if they wouldn't like to take over the defense of the village, and they say all right. So they start training together and living together and most important, they share danger, so they create a bond, and before you know it, they become a class—the professional warrior class—and the next thing you know, we're all civilians. What's more, these guys are not going to do that for nothing, and as the centuries go by, more and more of our surplus is going to pay off the war-riors, the "protectors."

After a few dozen centuries of this, we are all orga-nized into classes, with the warriors at the top, then the priests and scholars who rationalize the system, then the merchants and bankers who pay the warriors, then the craftsmen who provide armor for the warriors and goods for the merchants, then the farmers and workers, now called peasants and churls, and at the bottom the serfs and slaves. The class walls are so rigid now that your fate is sealed at birth: if your dad is a shepherd or a shoemaker, you'll be a shepherd or a shoemaker, because that is your "nature." If you wanted to be a hero, but your dad was not of the warrior class, you were out of luck. Forgotten were the days of our great, great, great . . . grandfathers, the first 39,600 of them, when, because bare survival was a close thing, every man counted, and every man was valued for his skill and courage, his savvy and honor, not for his birth and his social class. There was now so much surplus that a man's heroism could be expendable.

And it all happened so gradually that nobody remembered that it happened; it seemed like this was the way things had always been, and in the Middle Ages, ser-mons were preached about how God created these social classes, and you were sinful if you had any thoughts out-side of being in your social class.

So for most of 400 generations, this thing built up and got more and more rigid until it reached its height in the Middle Ages, and then it began to come apart. The first beginnings of the coming apart happened in the Renaissance, when men began to talk about "the dignity of man." But it didn't really get started until the end of the 18th century with the American Revolution and its Declaration of Independence ("all men are created equal") followed soon by the French Revolution ("liberty, fraternity, equality").

Then for over a hundred years followed by revolutions—democratic and nationalist—throughout Europe and the world. In the U.S., a great Civil War to put an end to the slave class. At the beginning of this century in Japan, the Bakufu finally fell, the political order that had propped up the samurai in power, and Japanese men greeted each other in the streets joyfully saying, "We are all samurai now.'"

In developing countries, this century has seen the crumbling of political colonialism, another form of feudalism with its rigid class structure.

In our own country, the Declaration of Independence and the American Revolution set the stage, but classism, the notion that a man is judged by his birth or wealth or social status instead of by his ideals and his qualities, still hung on pretty tight in some parts of the country. The South tried to remain as feudal as it could for as long as it could. Basically, what the South did was to import the model of the medieval knight errant and turn him into the chivalrous Southern gentleman. They had tournaments where these gentlemen would mount on horses and ride with their lances and try to lance the rings that were hanging from the poles, and they had their ladies' handkerchiefs tied around the lances, and the ladies were sitting over in the gallery and cheering their heroes because they read their Walter Scott novels and they knew how to do things medieval. And the whole show was propped up on the labor of the slave class.

But out in the West, men found themselves in a situation unlike any we'd known for 400 generations, ever since the surplus built up and the population began to swell: once again there was a whole lot more land than men. And as it was a dangerous and challenging land, good men were needed and were valued for their abilities. Instead of sorting men out by birth, wealth, or education, the frontier sorted men out by this one single big question:

Can you count on him?

Does he stand for something? And will he come through? This is the criterion by which all the frontier stories sort men out, and men fell into one of three groups:

> Heroes stand for ideals and have the right qualities; you can count on them.
> Villains don't stand for much beside themselves.
> Cowards are well meaning but won't be there for the showdown.

After 400 generations (a mere hiccup in our long history), manhood returns to the old universal criterion of our most ancient forefathers: a man's a man not from birth or wealth or status, but if you can count on him, if he has the ideals and the qualities that make him welcome in the great community of men.

Now the frontier is gone, the glorious wide-open spaces, and men mourn, and go back to the shop and the office. All, that is, except those who discover new frontiers. Wherever peace is threatened, or justice, or freedom—and they are always threatened by fear and greed, by child abuse and social injustice, by racism, sexism, homophobia, classism, and ageism, by violence, crime, and war, by ecological abuse—there men will begin to gather, a few at first, and then more and more, because in the places where the real work is done, and the real fight is fought, and the real life is lived, that's where nobody cares about your status or your fashionable clothes. They want to know what you stand for, what you can do, and can they count on you. That's the life that 40,000 grandfathers have prepared us to live.

Why Men Get So Tough

Why Men Get So Tough

Advancing into battle, Erik takes a spear in his thigh, pauses to pull it out, then hurls it back at its owner.

At supper, after a battle, Snorri's friends ask him why he's not eating much and Snorri says, "Lambs gagged for weaning are usually poor eaters." His friend reaches over, feels his throat, and finds an arrowhead embedded in the base of Snorri's tongue. He pulls it out, and Snorri is able to take his supper.

A razor-sharp sword slices down in front of Helgi's face and cuts off his bottom lip. Helgi looks at the enemy swordsman and says, "My face was never handsome, and you have done little to improve it." Then he takes his beard, clenches it in his teeth to stanch the wound, and goes to the attack.

If you had been a Viking boy ten centuries ago, you'd have grown up on stories like these, and practiced them over and over in play with your friends until you were old enough to go out and prove you could do it for real. You'd also have learned how to die from stories like these:

Thorgrim is sent forward to reconnoiter the area around Gunnar's house. Turning a corner, he takes a halberd in the stomach. He turns and walks back to his comrades, who ask, "Is Gunnar at home?" "His halberd certainly is," says Thorgrim, and falls dead at their feet.

Entering a hostile building, Atli takes a spear right through his middle, remarks to a friend, "The broad-bladed spear points seem to be in fashion these days," and falls across the doorsill.

John Wayne, eat your heart out. Ernest Hemingway, you was just a puppy.

The thing about Vikings, though, was that this was not just in battle—they tended to be this way most of the time. Two sworn-brothers, Thormod and Thorgeir, are out in the hills looking for an herb called angelica. Thorgeir has gone higher up the hill and Thormod is lower down, working along a ledge with a sheer drop-off way down to some rocks. A rock gives way and his foot slips and down he goes to certain death, but he grabs hold of a big bunch of angelica and hangs there.

His situation is such that he can't pull himself back up, and the roots are starting to give way, and he can't call out for help because that would be a weakness in a Viking. After a while his sworn-brother, Thorgeir, calls down, "Do you have enough angelica yet?" and Thormod calls back up, "I think I shall have enough when the one is gone which I am holding on to."

This sounds a little suspicious to Thorgeir, so he comes down and just in the nick of time he pulls his sworn-brother back up to the ledge. And then?—the two men never mention the incident again.

Where do these men come from? I guess they all come from little boys, but if Viking boys are like boys everywhere, and why wouldn't they be, what happens to make them like this?

A Viking was killed and his brothers are sitting at home talking about what needs to be done to avenge the family honor. It's a difficult situation involving political alliances among powerful families and it's not clear what to do and they talk it over. Time goes by and they are still talking it over. One evening they go in to supper and their mother serves them each a bowl of soup, and they look in the bowl and see boiling water poured over stones. They look at her and she looks at them and says, "You have swallowed worse things." The brothers are soon armed and riding.

Viking sagas are unique in the history of heroic literature in being mostly family sagas, so we get to see what happens in the home far more than in any other culture. We get hints of home life elsewhere (for example, the samurai saying that the three most alarming phenomena are fire, earthquake, and father), but no other culture gives us such a picture window into the interior scenes like Mother's Soup, and so nowhere else is it so clear that the motivation for this extreme macho life is shame and the fear of more shame.

There was a man called Thorarin, a man of peace, who just wanted to farm his farm and raise his family and not have any trouble. This got him a reputation for being weak, and a gang of bullies in the neighborhood decided that they would try to take his farm away from him. You need a pretext in Viking society, so they rode over and they said, "We think you've got some of our horses on your land and we're going to search." Thorarin, standing outside his house, says, "Do you have a warrant?" and they say, in the manner of bullies everywhere, "No, we don't have a warrant. You gonna try to stop us?" Thorarin knows the horses aren't there, so he says, "Go ahead," and goes back inside his house.

His mother has been standing inside listening, and when he walks in she says, "It's true what they say, you're more like a woman than a man, putting up with these insults. I don't know what I ever did to have a son like you." Thorarin arms, rides out, challenges the bully to a battle. In the fight, he cleaves the bully's skull down to the jaw, and the rest of the gang run away.

Thorarin rides home, tells his mother what he's done, and she says, "My words gave you an edge, then."

Viking mothers have a special niche in the Heroes' Hall of Fame, but no monopoly on shaming, which is epidemic in the culture. The sagas are mostly about endless family feuds and blood revenges and what they called family honor. Except that honor didn't mean an inner sense of rightness, it meant reputation. It meant what-will-people-say?, as Viking family meetings make clear. Never was a people more sensitive to the neighbors' gossip, or more touchy about taunts and dares. In some parts of Vikingdom, if a man made a shaming joke about you, and he told it to his friends and they all laughed, you could ride over and put that man to the sword, and then you could put all his friends to the sword for laughing, and here's the amazing part—although Viking culture had a strong legal system, and certain kinds of killings were punished severely—your revenge for the joke would be regretted but understood and allowed, because everybody knew that a Viking's honor can not stand being laughed at.

Arnkel, now an old man, is taunted and teased by a gang of 15 bullies. He arms himself and walks out into his death battle.

Nearly all Viking sagas are tragedies, and the real tragedy is that most Vikings were men of peace, who just wanted to farm their farms and raise their families. But

sooner or later, somebody would move into the neighborhood named Grim the Fierce, and then there would
be an incident, and then words and taunts, and then
reprisals, and then a killing, and then another. The list
would be long of the names of men who tried to live lives
of peace but were drawn into senseless feuds and wars by
taunting and the fear of shame.

It's not just the Vikings. Old Homer's heroes urge
each other into the battle, saying, "Let shame be in your
hearts," and there's the legendary story of the Spartan
mother who told her son before the battle, "Come home
with your shield or on it." (The dead were carried home
on their shields; cowards dropped their shields and ran.)

Bakaridjan, the greatest of all the heroes of the
African kingdom of Segu, backs away from a fight that
means certain death. Avoided by many, and teased by
the children in the streets, he withdraws, goes into a
deepening depression, and nears death from shame. Only
when his friends contrive a situation for him to be brave
again does he come back to life.

Any time a knight of the Round Table was unde-
cided about what to do, he would take council with his
friends, and if a fellow knight said, as they often did,
"'Twere great shame wert thou not to answer such a challenge as this," then that settled it. Anything but shame.

How many westerns have we seen where the
shoot-out begins with a taunt, or where a man (Gary
Cooper in *High Noon*, and many others) will walk out
into his death battle before he'll be shamed?

In Japan, the *Budo Shoshinshu*, the sixteenth-century Code of the Samurai, has these words: "both in doing right and in producing valor, there is no other way but a sense of shame."

"No other way"? As though we men didn't have enough native intelligence and enough natural integrity and courage to know and do the right thing. That view of us—that we need to be shamed—is so colossally, preposterously wrong-headed, not to mention counter-productive, that it makes you wonder how it could ever have gotten started.

It is such a disaster that I imagine that it came about in disastrous times, over long periods of pre-history, in the times of the highest danger, when the very survival of the tribe was threatened by invasion. The situation was desperate, and the thinking was desperate:

> For the sake of the survival of our whole tribe, our whole culture, we cannot have men who are afraid to fight or we will all die. How are we going to do this? What is stronger than fear? Ah, shame is stronger than fear. Even the fear of death.
>
> And you can't start too early. As the twig is bent, so grows the tree. Shame out of that boy any first sign of weakness, fear, cowardice, awkwardness, clumsiness, stupidity. All our lives depend on it.

I am beginning to think of the shaming of boys not just as a pattern in a dysfunctional family, but as a broad cultural pattern for training warriors who will respond to danger without thought of self-preservation.

Warriors it produces, but what kind of men? Shaming produces men who will fight and kill and be killed not for a just and noble cause, but for a taunt or a dare or a fear of the neighbors' gossip. Shame is that strong. A man who can be taunted is an open wound of shame.

The more macho the man, the more the boy was shamed. Death Before Dishonor means Death Before (any more of that worse-than-death) Shame. Death Before Dishonor. I had it tattooed on my arm in a desperate (and failed) attempt to show the world I was a man, and to escape the shame.

When my mother was a little girl, her mother locked herself and the children in the storm cellar with an arsenal because Pancho Villa was raiding in the territory and my grandfather had ridden out scouting. My mother watched her brothers being raised to be men who could respond instantly without fear of death should Pancho Villa and his men come riding over the hill, or cattle rustlers, or horse thieves, or whatever. That's how my mother learned how to raise boys.

And no matter how many generations we are removed from the frontier, or from the heroic age of our culture, these ways of training boys can be passed on and on and on, it may be for hundreds of thousands of years. It may make a difference in the way some of us look at our parents if it was not just them, but if they were acting out this broad and ancient cultural pattern which was designed maybe a million years ago to preserve our culture and save all our lives.

Well, it worked, since we're all here. But it sure is a relief to hear more and more men today talking about how the system may not be necessary, that just maybe we were brave and strong and smart and honorable all along, and the shaming didn't make us better men or better soldiers, it just made us numb and alcoholic and crazy.

Among the Vikings, where shaming is epidemic, the whole culture looks depressed, alcohol consumption is prodigious, and the level of violence is nearly psychotic. Our own culture is not without these signs.

Sometimes I talk with men who tell me they're grateful for the whippings and shamings because without them they figure they'd be lazy and useless, and maybe even evil. But that just sounds to me like more of the shaming.

What makes my heart jump up is when a man tells me he's overcome enough of his own shame to stop shaming his children. Even a million-year-old buck has to stop somewhere, and it looks like we're the generations who are starting to do it.

False Trails for Heroes

False Trails for Heroes

All the models of heroic tradition that have come down to us from all the different cultures make up a bewildering maze of trails—some true and some false. It's a lot easier to stay on the main path of heroic qualities in the service of ideals if we can recognize a false trail when we see it.

One false trail we have already seen is the business of total emotional containment. Nothing against emotional containment, which is a useful skill; it's that word, "total," which never allows a man to cry or show fear or get mad, that is sapping our strength .

A second false trail we've looked at is the wretched business of shaming boys and making them believe they're no good and will never accomplish anything if they don't keep on shaming themselves for the rest of their lives.

As I look at the whole picture, I see five more false trails that sap our strength, make fools of us, and keep us caged up away from reaching our highest goals.

1. *The Lone Wolf*. In Louis L'Amour's *Hondo*, (the best book John Wayne ever read), Hondo, when we first meet him, rides with his dog, Sam, up to a cabin where a woman is living out in the desert in Apache country alone with her young son. She serves a meal and when she goes to give Sam a scrap, Hondo stops her, saying:

> *"Sam's independent. He doesn't need anybody. I
> want him to stay that way. It's a good way."*
>
> *He helped himself to another piece of meat, to
> more potatoes and gravy.*
>
> *"But everyone needs someone."*
>
> *"Yes, ma'am. Too bad isn't it."*
>
> *She was puzzled by him, and yet there was a curi-
> ous attraction, too.*

With that last line, we become aware that we are now in
macho fantasyland. And sure enough it's only three pages
later that we get the line:

> *He made her feel like a woman.*

I grew up trying to be a Hondo type, and I never
understood why my relationships with women were so
distant and confusing and unsuccessful and agonizing.

The Lone Wolf, the Hondo-man, is so common
in our western fiction and comic books that he appears
to be the main type of man. But in the real heroic tradition he is harder to find. What we get much more com-
monly is the warrior *band.* The war *party,* the hunting
party. "All for one and one for all," said the Three Musketeers. Even in the stories of King Arthur, when a
knight rides out on a single quest, it's always a quest
that's appropriate to a single man. If it's against an army
or something larger than one giant or dragon, always you
take as many men as you need. Celtic warriors worked
in bands, and would often "take council" with each
other. Native American warriors made decisions in
democratic councils.

From the African heroic tradition come these words:

Heroism by itself brings trouble. It is not fitting to say, "I alone and nobody else am strong."

The world is made of mutual aid. He who helps another will be helped in turn.

Even if you become a warrior and surpass others, you will not fail to encounter the one who will grind your bones.

Sometimes people think that this Lone Wolf, this rugged individual came from the American frontier. But in fact, that is not the case. The pioneers were unquestionably rugged, and they were individualistic, they were highly self-dependent, and in general they shared a philosophy of live-and-let-live. But when the first wave of pioneers came over the Alleghenies and down into Kentucky and Tennessee, the first thing they did was to build a blockhouse for communal protection. And then they began the house raisings and the barn raisings, all done communally. Planting and harvesting were all communal. If somebody was sick, everybody helped out. If there was a fire, everybody came running. You cannot read the reminiscences of the pioneers without being overwhelmed with the picture that the west, the frontier, was settled by cooperation and teamwork, not by lone wolves.

Now somebody might say: well, this is the second wave of pioneers, and these men came with their families, so they had to be more communal, but the scouts and the mountain men, that's where you find the real rugged individuals, lone wolves. But that's not true either. All the mountain men had compañeros, or they lived with the native tribes. Of course, it's also true that the more men working a single stream, the fewer beaver to go around, so they tended to spread out a little, but they were always in twos or threes, and that was in friendly territory—Crow or Snake. If you went into Blackfoot territory, it was always with at least two dozen men who stayed close together. What's more, the camps were run communally. The men who were the best trappers spent the day out trapping. Two men stayed in to skin and cure the pelts. The men who were the best hunters spent the day out hunting to bring in supper. Two men guarded and cared for the stock. One man guarded and bossed the camp. When the expedition was over, all the pelts and all the profits were shared communally.

When you do find one of those legendary lone wolves like Old Bill Williams, they generally turn out to be half crazy, and even Old Bill spent the majority of his time with compañeros. And how did these men spend the Wyoming winters? All together, sometimes as many as 600 of them, camped in a valley, sharing whatever they had. They were, after all, in business, and lone wolfing was not good business.

OK, but what about the cowboys? Weren't they rugged individuals, lone wolves? In fiction, maybe, but in fact it would be hard to imagine anything more communal than a roundup and a trail drive, and men were hired on the basis of their ability to work as a team. If you were hiring and you needed 15 men for your outfit, 200 would show up, because everybody wanted to go on the drives, so you could choose men who worked well with each other.

And on the drives, most of the time you weren't within talking distance when you were working, but when you did come back around the campfire and you weren't too tired, what you generally got was a lot of horsing around and practical jokes and dares and tall tales and stories and songs around the campfire.

The impression you get from the journals of the real cowboys is that basically these guys were having the time of their lives. They were mostly in their teens and twenties, and a great number of them grew up picking cotton, which is backbreaking work that leaves you at the end of the day with your fingers shredded and your knees raw and with just about enough money for your supper. Then about the time you're 15 or 16 years old, you hear that somebody is going to pay you four times as much money for riding around all day on a big old horse? You get that job and you think you've died and gone to heaven, and all you want to do is be part of this group of men.

My opinion is that if one of these fictional Hondo types showed up in a real cow camp, he would have been regarded as standoffish, which would have made him a prime target for practical jokes.

What's more, cooperation wasn't just within the outfit. All the outfits on the trail helped each other as much as they could. Rustlers or horse thieves? There was a communal search. A man in trouble? Everybody rode to help. A river too swollen to cross without more men?

Everybody helped every herd across before anybody moved on. There was no race to beat somebody to market.

Get away from the fiction, the TV, and the comic books, and read the reminiscences of the real pioneers, mountain men, and cowboys, and the impression is overwhelming that the West was scouted and settled not by Lone Wolves, but by cooperation and teamwork.

The real origin of the Lone Wolf seems to be not in heroic tradition or in the reality of the West, but in a nineteenth century philosophy called Social Darwinism. It's a spinoff of Darwin's theory applied to human societies which says that human life all boils down to a

1. Struggle Against Nature for the
2. Survival of the Fittest in a
3. Ruthless Competition between
4. Rugged Individuals.

This theory was not thought up by anybody who was actually living out in nature on the frontier, because they were all too busy with the many communal jobs it took to live there. It was thought up by British professors sitting in armchairs, and soon became the darling of the nineteenth century robber baron capitalists who used it to justify any outrage of selfish greed. There are indications that the image of the Rugged Individual in fiction was financed by robber baron money.

By the 1890s, Social Darwinism was on the wane as a credible philosophy, but the image of the Lone Wolf, that rugged individual, was firmly entrenched in lore and fiction, where it still remains through sheer inertia, not because it tells us anything historically true or useful.

It also harms us. When I was a boy, I thought Roy Rogers and Hopalong Cassidy were pretty neat, but I was in absolute awe of The Lone Ranger. I sent in untold numbers of boxtops to get rings and secret codes and anything at all to get me feeling closer to that Man. Unconsciously, I grew up to be like him: psychologically masked, emotionally nonexistent; riding off into the distance. I got so wrapped up in the *style* of The Lone Ranger that I skipped right over the *substance*: the dedication to peace and justice, and laying his life on the line to serve the people. The "Lone" part of it was a false trail I took because I was ashamed and scared. It's a lot better these days with real compañeros, with less style and more substance.

2. *Flawlessness.* The image of the perfect hero who never makes a mistake is a very thin stream in the broad river of heroism. I can not find it anywhere in Asia or Africa or Native America, and I can not find it in Europe before the twelfth century. That's when Chretien de Troyes and numerous other writers began writing the romances that described a culture which was an interweaving of the old heroism with a certain variety of Christianity. In these new kinds of heroic stories, a hero's achievements are valued or ranked not only according to how much prowess and courage and savvy and honor they take, but also now according to their religious significance.

In this ranking, the highest of all the quests is the quest for the Holy Grail, and no knight can accomplish that quest unless he be "without sin, stain or vice." Naturally, that left a whole lot of guys out right off the bat. Only five knights ever made it very far. Sir Lancelot and Sir Gawain actually made it to The Chapel Perilous, but at the last minute some of their sins were recalled and they didn't even get to see the Holy Grail. Sir Lancelot wept bitterly over his failure and his sins. Two knights made it to the Chapel and actually got to see the Holy Grail. They were Sir Perceval and Sir Bors. But at the last minute, each of them had a tiny sin of omission and they failed.

Only one knight there was, who was without sin, stain or vice, and that was Sir Galahad, who saw the Grail and was transported to the Holy Land, being way too good for this world. Much has been made of Sir Galahad in certain traditions, notably Tennyson in his *Idylls of the King*, which dominated our country's heroic consciousness in the late Victorian Age. Some of us received this image of flawlessness from our Victorian grandparents; others got it from the endless run of stories of heroes who never made mistakes.

But really, in heroism worldwide, flawlessness is a very thin stream. What is much more typical of heroism, just to give one example from Nyangaland in eastern Zaire, is the story of Mwindo, who was the great culture hero of his people. Mwindo defeated dragons and sorcerers, and he journeyed to the land of the dead. With rattles and drums, he ascended to the sky on bridges built by Spider and walked with the clouds and the moon.

Smashed back to earth by Lightning, he laid his body down on the fire and had it forged into iron so that spears and knives broke on his skin. Then he challenged Lightning again, fought, and won.

But this same Mwindo, in the long course of his life, also boasts and fails, abandons his men, hides behind his sister, brews 2,000 quarts of beer, gets his face smashed into a tree, and craps in his pants. Now there's a hero we can identify with. And all in all, he kills off all the monsters and restores peace and order to his people, who love him for who he is.

Another one is Trickster, hero of a cycle of stories from the Winnebago tribe in this country. Trickster spends nearly all his time, story after story, in hilarious escapades trying to satisfy his hunger and sex drives. It looks like that's all his life is about. But then at last he remembers: Earthmaker had sent him here to earth for a reason. He had just forgotten. So he clears out all the obstacles to the people along the Mississippi River and kills all the bad spirits, so the people can live in peace and harmony. He ends up a great hero.

But many of us did not grow up on Trickster and Mwindo. We got latter-day versions of Sir Galahad, who appears everywhere in our culture. There was a man named Meriwether Lewis, who was co-commander of the Lewis and Clark Expedition. He has been out for a year and a half of adventure, and also of cold, hunger, sickness, encounters with hostile natives, facing down a grizzly bear with nothing in his hands but a halberd. He is President Jefferson's personal envoy to all the tribes, which in those days were regarded as sovereign, independent nations, and he has responsibility for this entire expedition of 40 men.

For the last few weeks, he's been searching the high mountains for the Shoshone, who have the horses to trade without which he can't go on. He climbs up to the Continental Divide, where no white man has ever been before, and walks unarmed into a camp of Shoshone. And what do you suppose he wrote in his journal on such a day? He wrote:

> *Today I passed my thirty first year . . . and I reflected that I had as yet done but little, very little, indeed, to further the happiness of the human race, or to advance the information of the succeeding generation. I viewed with regret the many hours I have spent in indolence and now sorely feel the want of that information which those hours would have given me had they been judiciously expended. But since they are passed and cannot be recalled, I dash from me the gloomy thought, and resolve in future to redouble my exertions to at least endeavor to ... promote human existence by giving ... the talents which nature and fortune have bestowed upon me; or, in future, to live for mankind, as I have heretofore lived for myself.*

Well, he's only 31. What do you say we give him another chance?

No matter what you do, it's a failure if it's not flawless. It's pretty good, Lancelot maybe, but not up to Galahad. There's a tiny stain, weep for your sins.

One of the difficulties with trying to be flawless is that you can never admit a mistake, so you can never apologize and be forgiven, so your mind is taken up with endless justifications of the past instead of creative plans for the future. A second difficulty is that the essential quality of savvy is gained from the experiences of trial and error, and if we have to be flawless, we'll be too frozen to take risks and learn savvy.

A final difficulty is that aspirants to flawlessness don't usually have a real terrific sense of humor about themselves. One of the great attributes of the heroes of our frontier was a self-effacing humor. In the first half of the nineteenth century, it was overstated ("I'm half horse and half alligator with a touch o' the snappin' turtle. I can ride a streak o' lightnin' and whip my weight in wildcats.") Later, the style changed to understated ("Aw, shucks, ma'am, 'twaren't nothin'.") But these are both ways of laughing at ourselves, and that's a good quality in a hero because it keeps him human. It's one of the saving graces of John Wayne. Highly recommended for sufferers from flawlessness.

3. *Courage in a Bottle.* This is a story well known, well told by many, and it doesn't need me to repeat it: how alcohol can give us a little courage at first, but then starts to sap our energy.

Another thing about heroes is that we love adventure, love a challenge, and this has to do with our personal energy. Sometimes I hear people say that we men are naturally "aggressive," because of testosterone or whatever. But that word means anger and hostility, and I wish people would stop saying we're aggressive, and say instead that testosterone makes us bold and adventurous.

Anyway, we do love adventure and challenge of some kind or other—physical, emotional, mental, or spiritual—just as long as we have the personal energy for it, and when a man loses that love it's because something is draining his energy, and alcohol will do that sooner or later. I don't believe there are enough data in existence to really pin this down, but the subjective impression I get from all my reading is that the more shaming there is in a culture and the more macho, the more the men drink. In the Viking stories, there's beer for breakfast, and drinking contests just to see who can drink the most before they pass out. These are not 15-year-old boys, these are men in their twenties and thirties. The only two cultures I have found to compare with it are the Russian and our own.

In Russia, there's a whole cycle of epic stories built around the theme of the feast. At this huge feast, you see how much you can eat, and then you see how much you can drink. Then, when everybody is really liquored up, you have a boasting contest to see who can boast the greatest boast. That's not so bad, except that the next day you have to do what you boasted. Can you imagine waking up with your head pounding and you can hardly see through your swollen eyes, and your friends come in smiling and tell you that this is the day you ride out against the Dragon of the North. ("I said what?!")

It's funny the first time.

4. *Rescuing Damsels.* Wherever a hero is battling the forces of chaos and injustice, he is doing this to protect the women, along with the children and elders, the village, the land, and the culture. That's always his job. But this stuff where the hero's main business is to ride out and rescue a damsel from some giant or other, and then marry her—I can't find this in the old heroic stories from Asia, or Africa, or Native America, and I can't find it in Europe before the 12th century. Rescuing damsels was not part of the old heroic traditions.

But just about that time in France, the ladies of the courts had begun to achieve lives of some leisure, and poets discovered that here was an eager and wealthy audience for tales that focused the men's energies on women. That was the birth of a new kind of story called the "romance," and there seemed to be no end to people's appetite for tales of rescuing.

Romances gained an enormous popularity in the early 19th century when they poured from the pen of Sir Walter Scott and his legion of emulators, including Alexander Dumas and James Fenimore Cooper, who lifted Scott's plots and transplanted them to the United States, so instead of knights and lairds rescuing damsels and lassies from the castles of wicked lords, Leatherstocking and the good Indians rescue fair maidens from wicked Indians atop rocky palisades, which was as close as Cooper could come to a castle in his neck of the woods. From Cooper there flows a stream so broad—into fiction, film, and TV—of heroes rescuing damsels from distress that you would think heroes seldom did much else.

Of course, the real reason for so much damsel rescuing is that if you write a tale of men having adventures, mostly men will read it, but if the object of the man's energies is a woman, then women will also read it, and you have doubled your readers, your sales, and your income. Why not?

The effect of this on our psyches is something else. The more we adopt the rescuer approach toward women, the more we need women who are rescuable, meaning helpless and pathetic, and we are shocked to read in Viking sagas of women who in the 10th century controlled their own property, divorced their husbands at will, and sometimes fought alongside their men, dealing out some vicious blows with swords and axes.

Never has one group of people (men) been fed so many dopey generalizations about another group of people (women). (Unless it's all the dopey generalizations women are fed about us.) The truth about women is that when they're fully themselves, and not being rescuees, either wilting under it or resenting it or both, they're smart and capable and tremendously fun to have as real, whole partners. Also, nothing about ideals and qualities like courage and honor is outside of womanhood, and with women beside us, we can double the number of heroes we have to fight the good fights.

But rescuing damsels will always appeal to a man who's had his pride taken away, and he doesn't believe he could really be loved, so he'll settle for Gratitude. The contract is: I rescue you from your father, from your ex-husband (the dragon, the wicked lord), from your poverty, from your alcohol or drug addiction, from your depression, from whatever distress you're in, and then you owe me forever and ever. Some really horrendous marriages come out of that.

Rescuing damsels is not heroic. It's romantic, which is very different. Heroes, both men and women, have lots of good things to be doing.

5. *Villainizing.* The last of the false trails is turning another man (or woman) into a villain so we can look like a hero. This is everywhere. Our leaders do it to other countries' leaders. They do it to each other. We do it to our leaders. We do it to each other. And it's just devastating. It alienates us from each other. It seems to justify not just minimum necessary force for restraint, but any degree of violence against the person we see as a villain. It puts all the blame over there (on them, on her, on the government, or whoever) so we stay stuck in some comic book hero image we picked up 20, 30, 40 years ago, and we don't have to look at ourselves and get real. This is devastating.

But then doesn't every story we grew up on have a villain? Doesn't fighting a villain define a hero? How can we be heroes if there aren't any villains to fight? If we're going to practice our courage and savvy and prowess and honor, who are we going to practice it on? And aren't there actual villains who have to be stopped?

The real villains are not Whos but Whats. Here's a villain: a chemical addiction. That's one that takes all our skill and courage to defeat. If we don't have any more of those, here's another villain: a psychological addiction. Watching TV and munching stuff. Working week-ends at jobs we don't even like. Spending the evenings figuring out how to get in bed with the next woman. Those are villains because they rob the world of a hero, and fighting them takes all our savvy and skill and courage and honor. Every man knows what his own villains are.

The greatest epics in all our traditions show that the first step in heroism is self-mastery. In the *Iliad*, Achilles must master his anger, which he's unable to do until he finds compassion for the enemy. In the *Odyssey*, Odysseus can't return from long exile to cleanse his home of villains until he satisfies the gods that he's cleansed himself of his own arrogance and villainy which got him lost in the first place. Self-mastery. From an African heroic tale comes this conclusion:

> *Let a man not say that he is overcoming someone else, but that he is overcoming himself.*

In this same African culture, they have a tradition that a man first becomes a warrior, and as a warrior he is passionate, ambitious, reckless, challenging, fighting, destroying. He has not yet received the teachings. Only when a warrior has been through enough ordeals and hardships and tests does he learn to respect people, and when he respects people, then he becomes a chief. The job of the chief is to think and work for the peace and harmony of the tribe. The chief does not go out on the hunt, and he never kills an animal, not even an insect.

There's another tradition in the Winnebago tribe in this country: the chief never goes to war, but his job is to work for peace and harmony, and to plead for mercy for the offender.

The greatest of the medieval tales are the Quests for the Holy Grail, and even to begin on such an adventure, a knight must spend months or years in purification of himself. The purifications release and give back to him the energies that were swallowed up in maintaining his addictions and psychological patterns, energies he needs for his quest.

As self-mastery frees us up, all the energies we had devoted to our addictions and patterns expand and grow, filling us up until they begin to flow out onto the field of action. A man finds an arena that suits him, one with the villains he'd most like to vanquish: it could be war or crime; child abuse or social injustice; ecological abuse; racism, sexism, homophobia, classism, ageism (our fears of each other); or fear itself. These are the monsters and giants attacking the people, and we are the heroes to stop them.

A man mastering himself knows how to proceed. Uniting with his ideals and heroic qualities, he sloughs off his addictions and patterns. Sloughing off his addictions and patterns, he unites with his ideals and heroic qualities. The more he does this, the larger he becomes and the more he sees who he is; and the more he sees who he is, the more he sees the heroism in everyone.

The people are not the monsters. The monsters are the fears, and the addictive and abusive behaviors. The people are all our allies and fellow heroes, battling to conquer their own monsters, needing our aid and assistance, giving us theirs. For men finding self-mastery, this is a way of life.

All over the world, men are coming together; taking council with each other; sharing fears and tears and laughter; giving mutual aid and encouragement. We are leaving the false trails and finding the heart of the old traditions—ideals and courage and prowess and skill and savvy and honor—walking after the finest of our forefathers. Behind us, the boys of the rising generation are watching. My God, what a time to be alive!

Notes

Notes

p. v   This roll of heroes is as complete as I can reasonably make it, working within the confines of what has been translated into English. There are many great epics yet untranslated, from Polish, for example, and from several African languages.

p. 6   These stories about Davy Crockett are from the *Narrative of the Life of David Crockett*, "By Himself," pp. 28, 74, 102, 104.

Kit Carson's meeting with the bears is on p. 38 of his *Autobiography*.

p. 8   Sir Cologreant can be found in the story of "Yvain," *Arthurian Romances*, p. 184.

Bassadjalan Zambele is in *The Heart of the Ngoni*, p. 45.

p. 19   There is a great deal of valuable information about tears in *The Mystery of Tears*.

p. 20   The great scene with Priam and Achilles is in Book xxiv of *The Iliad*, 11. 476 ff.

These scenes of Odysseus are in *The Odyssey*, Book v, p. 85 and Book xvi, p. 295 f.

p. 21   The stories of Caesar and Alexander come from *Plutarch's Lives*, p. 499 and p. 464 ff.

p. 22   The grieving of Joshua is in the *Book of Joshua*, Chapter 7.

p. 22 The tale of Mercurius and "the gift of tears" is in *Medieval Russia's Epics*, pp. 208-10.

p. 23 Diuladjan's words are on pp. 166-67 of *The Heart of the Ngoni*.

p. 25 The story of the death of Crazy Horse is told in *Black Elk Speaks*, pp. 140-45.

Quetzalcoatl's tears are told in *Shaking the Pumpkin*, p. 119.

Martin Fierro's words are on p. 15 of *The Gaucho Martin Fierro*.

p. 26 The scenes from *Beowulf* are on p. 30 and p. 98.

p. 27 The fight between Sir Lancelot and Sir Tristram is from *Tales of King Arthur*, p. 120.

p. 28 David and Jonathan weep with each other in I Samuel 20.

Arthur and Owein embrace in the *Mabinogion*, p. 173.

p. 29 Siegfried is mourned on pp. 96 ff. of the *Nibelungenlied*.

The great lamentation is in *Aventiures* 37-39.

The two scenes from *The Song of Roland* are on p. 57 and pp. 79-80.

p. 30 The two scenes from *The Poem of the Cid* are on p. 37 and p. 63.

p. 31 Russian sobs like thunder are in *Russian Heroic Poetry*, p. 274.

The scenes from the *Kalevala* are on p. 101, v. 2 (Ilmarinen), pp. 64-5, v. 1 and pp. 166-67, v. 2 (Vainamoinen), and pp. 41-50, v. 2 (Lemminkainen).

p. 33 The medieval etiquette advice is quoted on p. 13 of *Rudeness and Civility*.

The information about the French salon comes partly from *An Introduction to Seventeenth Century France*, pp. 222 ff. and partly from my wife, Anya, a former professor of French.

p. 35 The words of the noble Lord Chesterfield are to be found in *Letters, Sentences and Maxims*, pp. 139-40, p. 216, and p. 215.

p. 36 Crusoe says this on p. 161 of *Robinson Crusoe*.

p. 38 Henty's biographer is quoted on p. 47 of *Written for Children*.

Buffalo Bill is thus described on p. 11 of *Buffalo Bill and His Adventures in the West*.

p. 39 These scenes from *The Virginian* are on p. 228 and p. 346.

p.40 Hondo is thus described on p. 5 of *Hondo*.

p. 42 These bitter lines from Dante are in Canto xxxiv of the *Inferno*.

p. 47 The description of Stone Age life is adapted from "The Original Affluent Society" in *Stone Age Economics*.

p. 49 The story of the origin and development of social classes is a dramatization of my memories of my lectures on Civilization, given at Austin College some 25 years ago.

p. 55 The story of Snorri is from the *Eyrbyggja Saga*, p. 150.

The story of Helgi's lip is told in the "Droplaugarsonasaga," p. 123. The line is quoted from the translation of Peter Hallberg in *The Icelandic Saga*, p. 115.

Thorgrim's death is told on p. 169 of *Njal's Saga*.

Atli's death is told in *The Icelandic Saga*, p. 98.

p. 56 The story of Thormod and Thorgeir is from *The Saga of the Sworn Brothers*, pp. 179-80.

"Mother's Soup" is a story retold in *The Icelandic Saga*, p. 120.

p. 57 The tale of Thorarin and his Mom is found in the *Eyrbyggja Saga*, pp. 64-68.

p. 58 Arnkel's death battle is told on p. 120 ff. of the *Eyrbyggja Saga*.

p. 59 The story of Bakaridjan is from *The Heart of the Ngoni*, pp. 127-45.

p. 60 These words from the *Budo Shoshinshu* are on p. 33.

p. 65 This Hondo and Sam story is on p. 15 of *Hondo*.

p. 67 The sayings from Africa are from *Hero and Chief*, p. 124.

p. 72   The stories of Mwindo are all found in *Hero and Chief*.

p. 73   The tale of Trickster is found in "The Winnebago Trickster Cycle," *American Indian Literature*.

p. 74   Meriwether Lewis' journal entry is on p. 241 of *The Journals of Lewis and Clark*.

p. 76   The Russian boasting stories are found in *The Epic Songs of Russia*.

p. 80   The words from Africa are on p. 150 of *Hero and Chief*.

Winnebago customs are described in "The Winnebago Trickster Cycle," *American Indian Literature*.

Bibliography and Films

Bibliography

The Ancient Western World

GREECE

The Iliad. Homer. trans. Richmond Lattimore. University of Chicago Press, 1965.

The Odyssey. Homer. trans. Robert Fitzgerald. University of Chicago Press, 1961.

Selected Lives and Essays. Plutarch. trans. John Langhorne. Neal, 1831.

ROME

The Aeneid. Virgil. trans. Robert Fitzgerald. Random House, 1984.

ISRAEL

The Bible (Joshua, Judges, I & II Samuel, I & II Kings, I & II Chronicles) RSV, trans. 1611. Oxford University Press, 1962

Western Europe

PORTUGAL

The Lusiads. Luis vaz de Camoens. trans. William. C. Atkinson. Penguin, 1952.

SPAIN

Poem of the Cid. trans. W. S. Merwin. New American Library, 1959

FRANCE

The Song of Roland. trans. W. S. Merwin. Vintage, 1963.

ITALY
The Divine Comedy. Dante. trans. John Ciardi. Norton. 1977

GERMANY
The Nibelungenlied. trans. D. G. Mowatt. Dent, 1965.
The Volsungasaga. trans. William Morris. Scott, Ltd., n.d.

ENGLAND
Beowulf. trans. David Wright. Penguin, 1983.

WALES
The Mabinogion. trans. Gwyn Jones & Thomas Jones. Dent, 1949.
The Gododdin. trans. Desmond O'Grady. Dolmen, 1977.

IRELAND
Early Irish Literature. ed. Myles Dillon. University of Chicago Press, 1948.
The Cuchullin Saga in Irish Literature. ed. Eleanor Hull. Nutt, 1898.

SCOTLAND
Heroic Poetry From The Book of the Dean of Lismore. ed. Neil Ross. Scottish Gaelic Texts Society, 1939.
The Bruce. John Barbour. MacLellan, 1964.

ARTHURIAN TALES
Tales of King Arthur. Sir Thomas Malory. ed. Michael Service. Schocken, 1989.
Perceval. Chretien de Troyes. trans. Ruth Cline. University of Georgia Press, 1985.
"Lancelot" and "Yvain" from *Arthurian Romances.* Chretien de Troyes. trans. W. W. Comfort. Dent, 1975.

Northern Europe

VIKING

Njal's Saga. trans. Magnus Magnusson & Hermann Palsson. Penguin, 1960.

Eyrbyggja Saga. trans. Hermann Palsson & Paul Edwards. University of Toronto Press, 1973.

Egil's Saga. trans. Christine Fell. Dent, 1975.

Vinland the Good: The Saga of Leif Eriksson and the Viking Discovery of America. trans. Joan Blindheim. Johan Forlag. Oslo, 1970.

The Saga of King Heidrik the Wise. trans. Christopher Tolkien. Nelson, 1960.

The Saga of Kormak and *The Saga of the Sworn Brothers*. trans. Lee Hollander. Princeton University Press, 1949

The Saga of the Jomsvikings. trans. N.F. Blake. Nelson, 1962.

The Laxdoela Saga. trans. A. M. Arent. University of Washington Press, 1964.

The Saga of Gunnlaug Serpent-Tongue. trans. R. Quirk. Nelson, 1957.

The Saga of the Faroe Islanders. trans. Muriel Press. Dent, 1934.

The Saga of Gisli. trans. George Johnston. Dent, 1963.

"Droplaugarsonasaga" from *Three Icelandic Sagas*. trans. Margaret Schauch. Princeton University Press, 1950.

The Icelandic Saga. Peter Hallberg. University of Nebraska Press, 1962.

FINLAND

Kalevala: Land of Heroes. trans. W.F. Kirby. Dent, 1923.

Eastern Europe

THE BALKANS

Marko the Prince. trans. Anne Pennington & Peter Levi. Duckworth, 1984.

The Battle of Kosovo. trans. John Matthias & Vladeta Vuckovic. Swallow, 1987.

RUSSIA

The Epic Songs of Russia. trans. Isabel Hapgood. Kraus, 1969.

Russian Heroic Poetry. trans. N. Kershaw Chadwick. Russell, 1964.

Medieval Russia's Epics, Chronicles and Tales. trans. Serge Zenkovsky. Dutton, 1974.

"Lay of the Host of Igor." from *A Treasury of Russian Literature*. trans. Bernard Guerney. Vanguard, 1943.

Asia

SUMERIA

The Epic of Gilgamesh. trans. N. K. Sandara. Penguin, 1972.

PERSIA

The Shah Nameh. Firdausi. trans. James Atkinson. London, 1882.

INDIA

The Mahabharata. trans. C. V. Narashiman. 1965.

The Ramayana. trans. Shudha Mazumdar. Orient Longman, 1974.

MONGOLIA

The Heroic Epic of the Khalka Mongols. Nichola Poppe. trans. from the Russian by J. Krueger, D. Montgomery, & M. Walton. The Mongolia Society, 1979.

JAPAN

The Code of the Samurai (Budo Shoshinshu). Daidoji Yuzan. trans. A. L. Sadler. Tuttle, 1988.

Tales of Samurai Honor (Buke Giri Monogatari). Ihara Sikaku. trans. Caryl Ann Callahan. Tokyo, 1981.

Tales of Times Now Past (from the *Konjaku Monogatari*). trans. Marian Ury. University of California Press, 1979.

Shomonki: The Story of Masakado's Rebellion. trans. Judith Rabinovitch. Monumenta Nipponica, 1986.

Tale of the Disorder in Hogen (Hogen Monogatari). trans. William. R. Wilson. Tokyo, 1971.

The Way of the Samurai. Richard Storry. Putnam's, 1978.

AINU (pre-Japanese inhabitants of the Japanese Islands)

Songs of Gods, Songs of Humans: The Epic Tradition of the Ainu. Donald L. Philippi. Princeton University Press, 1979.

Africa

MALI

The Heart of the Ngoni: Heroes of the African Kingdom of Segu. Harold Courlander, with Ousmane Sako. Crown, 1982.

ZAIRE

Hero and Chief. Daniel Buybieck. University of California Press, 1978.

SWAHILI

Epic Poetry in Swahili and Other African Languages. Jan Knappert. Brill, 1983.

Native America

Black Elk Speaks. as told to John G. Neihardt. University of
Nebraska Press, 1979.
"The Winnebago Trickster Cycle." *American Indian Literature:
An Anthology.* ed. Alan Velie . University of Oklahoma
Press, 1979.
"Quetzalcoatl: An Aztec Hero Myth." *Four Masterworks of Amer-
ican Indian Literature.* ed. John Bierhorst. Farrar, 1974.
*Shaking The Pumpkin: Traditional Poetry of the Indian North Amer-
icas.* ed. Jerome Rothenberg. Doubleday, 1972.
numerous hunting, war, and medicine songs from various
anthologies.

South America

CHILE
The Araucaniad. Alonso de Ercilla y Zuniga. trans. Charles Lan-
caster and Paul Manchester. Vanderbilt University
Press, 1945.

ARGENTINA
The Gaucho Martin Fierro. Jose Hernandez. trans. Frank Carrino.
Scholar's Facsimiles, 1974.

The Epic of Latin American Literature. Arturo Torres-Rioseco.
University of California Press, 1964.

Australia

The Speaking Land: Myth and Story in Aboriginal Australia. Ronald
and Catherine Bernt. Penguin, 1988.
The Australian Heroes. Geoffrey Dutton. Angus and Robertson,
1981.

The United States Frontier

EXPLORERS

The Journals of Lewis and Clark. ed. Frank Bergon. Viking, 1989.

The Journals of Zebulon Montgomery Pike. ed. Donald Jackson. University of Oklahoma Press, 1966.

FRONTIERSMEN AND MOUNTAIN MEN

A Narrative of the Life of David Crockett. Davy Crockett. Limbird, 1834.

Kit Carson's Autobiography. Kit Carson. ed. Milo Quaife. Lakeside, 1935.

Journal of a Mountain Man: James Clyman. ed. Linda Hasselstrom. Mountain Press, 1984.

The Life and Adventures of James P. Beckwourth, Mountaineer, Scout and Pioneer, and Chief of the Crow Nation of Indians. as told to T.D. Bonner. 1965.

Life in the Far West. George Frederick Ruxton. University of Oklahoma Press, 1979.

My Sixty Years on the Plains. W. T. Hamilton. Forest & Stream, 1905.

Journal of a Trapper. Osborne Russell. ed. Aubrey Haines. Oregon Historical Society, 1955.

Jedediah Smith and the Opening of the West. Dale Morgan. University of Nebraska Press, 1953.

Jim Beckwourth: Black Mountain Man and Crow War Chief. Elinor Wilson. University of Oklahoma Press, 1972.

Old Bill Williams: Mountain Man. Alpheus Favour. University of Oklahoma Press, Press, 1936.

Mody Boatright: Folklorist. ed. Ernest Speck. University of Texas Press, 1973.

COWBOYS

Log of a Cowboy. Andy Adams. Houghton Mifflin, 1903.

A Texas Cowboy, or, Fifteen Years on the Hurricane Deck of a Spanish Pony. Charlie Siringo. Umbdenstock, 1885.

Pioneer Days in the Southwest From 1850-1879. Charles Goodnight. Guthrie, Oklahoma, 1909.

Life in the Saddle. Frank Collinson. University of Oklahoma Press, 1963.

Twilight on the Range: Recollections of a Latterday Cowboy. William Timmons. University of Texas Press, 1962.

Ranch Life and the Hunting Trail. Theodore Roosevelt. St. Martin's Press, 1985.

Famous Gunfighters of the Old West. Bat Masterson. Weatherford, 1982.

The Eastern Establishment and the Western Experience: The West of Frederic Remington, Theodore Roosevelt and Owen Wister. G. Edward White. University of Texas Press, 1989.

Adventure Tales And Novels

THE 17TH AND 18TH CENTURIES

Pilgrim's Progress. John Bunyan. Revell, 1903.
Gulliver's Travels. Jonathan Swift. Nelson, 1940.
Robinson Crusoe. Daniel Defoe. Houghton Mifflin, 1908.

THE 19TH CENTURY

Waverly. Walter Scott. Black, 1829.
Ivanhoe. Walter Scott. Dent, 1959.
Rob Roy. Walter Scott. London, 1843.
The Talisman. Walter Scott. Dodd, Mead, 1943.
"Autobiography." *Memoirs of the Life of Sir Walter Scott.* Lockhart, 1837.
Sir Walter Scott. John Lander. Twayne, 1966.

The Three Musketeers. Alexander Dumas. Doubleday, 1952.

The Deerslayer. James Fenimore Cooper. Library of America, 1985.

The Last of the Mohicans. James Fenimore Cooper. Library of America, 1985.

The Pathfinder. James Fenimore Cooper. Library of America, 1985.

The Pioneers. James Fenimore Cooper. Library of America, 1985.

The Prairie. James Femimore Cooper. Library of America, 1985.

Twenty Thousand Leagues Under the Sea. Jules Verne. Dodd, Mead, 1952.

BOYS' FICTION
Treasure Island. Robert Louis Stevenson. Dent, 1962.

Kidnapped. Robert Louis Stevenson. American House, 1983.

Among the Redskins. William Kingston. Callell, n.d.

The Young Foresters & Other Tales. William Kingston. Miller, 1866.

The Golden Canyon. George A. Henty. Hurst, 1899.

Held Fast for England: G. A. Henty, Imperialist Boys' Writer. Guy Arnold. Hamilton, 1980.

Written for Children. John Rowe Townsend. Garnet Miller, 1965.

A Critical History of Children's Literature. Cornelia Meggs, *et al.* Macmillan, 1953.

THE DIME NOVELS
Buffalo Bill and His Adventures in the West. Ned Buntline. Arno, 1974.

Deadwood Dick, the Prince of the Road, or, The Black Rider of the Black Hills. Edward. L. Wheeler. Garland, 1979.

Seth Jones, or, The Captives of the Frontier. Edward S. Ellis. Garland, 1978.

THE TWENTIETH CENTURY
The Virginian. Owen Wister. Macmillan, 1929.
Riders of the Purple Sage. Zane Grey. Black, 1912.
Hondo. Louis L'Amour. Gregg, 1978.
Lonigan. Louis L'Amour. Bantam, 1988.

History of Men and Emotions

The Book of the Courtier. Baldesar Castiglione. trans. Charles Singleton. Anchor, 1959.
An Introduction to Seventeenth Century France. John Lough. Longmans, 1960.
Letters, Sentences and Maxims. Lord Chesterfield. Burt, New York, n.d.
Lord Chesterfield and His World. Samuel Shellabarger. Little, Brown, 1951.
Rudeness and Civility: Manners in Nineteenth-Century Urban America. John Kasson. Hill & Wang, 1990.
Crying: The Mystery of Tears. William H. Frey. Winston, 1985.

Other

Manliness and Morality: Middle Class Masculinity in Britain and America, 1820-1940. ed. J. A. Mangan & James Walvin. St. Martin's Press, 1987.
Stone Age Economics. Marshall Sahlins. Oldive, 1972.

Books About Films

Focus on the Western. ed. Jack Nachbar. Prentice-Hall, 1974.
John Wayne and the Movies. Allen Eyles. Grosset, 1976.
John Wayne: The Man/The Actor. George Bishop. House, 1979.

Films

JOHN WAYNE FILMS

OTHER

Stagecoach. 1939
The Spoilers. 1942
Fort Apache. 1948
Red River. 1948
She Wore a Yellow Ribbon. 1949
Rio Grande. 1950
The Searchers. 1956
Rio Bravo. 1959
The Horse Soldiers. 1959
North to Alaska. 1960
The Comancheros. 1961
The Man Who Shot Liberty Valance. 1962
The Sons of Katie Elder. 1965
El Dorado. 1967
The War Wagon. 1967
The Undefeated. 1969
True Grit. 1969
Chisum. 1970
Rio Lobo. 1970
Big Jake. 1971
The Cowboys. 1972
The Train Robbers. 1973
Cahill, United States Marshall. 1973
Rooster Cogburn. 1975
The Shootist. 1976

High Noon. Gary Cooper 1952

Acknowledgements

Ah, the professors of old—what giants of men they were: Mody Boatright, whose graduate courses on Folklore and on American frontier life first fired my imagination over 30 years ago; Wilson Hudson, whose courses on Epic Literature introduced me to Carl Jung and Joseph Campbell way back then; William Arrowsmith, who taught me how to read *The Iliad* and *The Odyssey* with soul and heart. God rest you, merry gentlemen.

I also wish to thank professor Bill Stott, whose erudition saved me many steps in the library; Lyman Grant for his firm editorial support; Terence Donahue, for his very timely help; all the guys who came to the workshop that started all this; and my wife, Anya, my pilgrim soul's true mate and lover.

About the Author

Dan Jones grew up in Texas and spent summers wrangling horses. After serving two years in the Marine Corps, he earned a Ph.D. in English and for 15 years taught courses in Western literature and civilization.

A counselor in Austin since 1978, he is the therapist featured in John Lee's *The Flying Boy*, and he was a "Representative Man" chosen by MAN! *Magazine*. He and John began leading men's groups together in 1986, and their work in and love for the men's movement continues to grow. Dan has been happily married for 19 years.